I Was a Mistake

Another Type of Abuse

Shawn Woods

authorHOUSE®

AuthorHouse™
1663 Liberty Drive
Bloomington, IN 47403
www.authorhouse.com
Phone: 1 (800) 839-8640

Published by AuthorHouse   07/17/2015

ISBN: 978-1-5049-2293-7 (sc)
ISBN: 978-1-5049-2292-0 (e)

Library of Congress Control Number: 2015911272

Print information available on the last page.

Dedication

I dedicate this book to my father who was a very devoted family man who gave up going to college and stayed home during the great depression and work to help support his father and mother his two brothers and one sister, plus join the Navy in WWII to fight for our country.

He thought me that working hard and learning to be dedicated to your family was the most important thing a young man could do with his life.

He also showed me that getting a good job and doing your best for who you work for was the most honorable thing a man could do even if the company you work for did not appreciate you or rewarded you for your efforts. But he did teach one very important thing and that you need to look out for number one you are the most important person so take care of yourself because no one will.

My father did not have I quite in his vocabulary he never gave up on anything he always found a way to make descent living to support his family and worked hard to give us everything he could.

His never give up attitude rubbed off on me and it made me a very strong willed individual in my life and when life knocked me down you always get up and went back at it harder and stronger, my father always showed me how to be a individual leader.

The most I learned from my father was you can fix anything yourself by taking it apart and repairing it yourself. When I got married and moved out on my own he was always there to talk to and ask for help if I needed him he would drop everything and come over to show me and be there to guide me on how to do it and help were needed.

The bond between a father and son is very unique and ours was so unique I cannot explain our bond, even to this day my wife does not understand how are bond was so strong, even my own children could understand what my father and I had and I could not explain it to them until they now see the bond we have together.

A simple smile, a look, a nod, or even a few word of encouragement meant more to me than anything else. My father was a very patient person and knew how to direct me and encourage me to a path of being a strong willed never give up man that into today's world nothing is easy and working hard and never give up attitude will keep you strong and let nothing in this world from knocking you down and keep you from getting up.

I have promised myself that as a father I would have as good or even better bond with my sons then I had with my father and be able teach my sons what my father has thought me and I believe that my son are even better than I am which they have showed me they are good hard working individuals who have succeed in school, work and in life and are very strong willed individuals.

Father made life bearable when it seemed as if nothing was going right he was there to talk to in his own way and was supportive in the things when I need it, but there were some flaws in him he was not perfect and who is, but I wish he was more around for me when I really needed him.

Chapter 1

INTRODUCTION

I understand there are worst things in life that what I have experienced and what other people have gone thru and a lot worst then I did, but this books is about my struggles with my personal issues were I developed learning disabilities at a very young age, and not able to develop a meaningful relationship with women, very low Self-esteem, no confidence in myself to try anything.

But this book is more of how I over came these issues and became a better person a successful person that I had to climbed and clawed my way up a corporate ladder made a good home for my children, built a developed my self-esteem with confidence to try anything and how you can put my mind to what you want to achieve and do it, this is why I am writing this book to inspire others to never give up on what your dream is, or your goal in life never quite

1

trying to succeed and how to be a better person no matter how many times you fail.

Just get up and start again, life will knock you down over and over again but you need to get up and keep trying and you can succeed in life, but you have to work hard for what you want. This is my story and this is why I am writing it, this will be a challenge because of my disabilities I write and read at a 6 and 8 grade level I will do my best and try to get my point across.

Let's look at the word **a·buse** and the definition of this word.

Synonyms

1. misapply. **2.** ill-use, maltreat, injure, harm, hurt. **3.** vilify, vituperate, berate, scold; slander, defame, calumniate, traduce. **6.** misapplication. **7.** slander, aspersion. ABUSE, CENSURE, INVECTIVE all mean strongly expressed disapproval. ABUSE implies an outburst of harsh and scathing words against another (often one who is defenseless): *abuse directed against an opponent.* CENSURE implies blame, adverse criticism, or hostile condemnation: *severe censure of acts showing bad judgment.* INVECTIVE applies to strong but formal denunciation in speech or print, often in the public interest: *invective against graft.*
to use wrongly or improperly; misuse: *to abuse one's authority.*
to treat in a harmful, injurious, or offensive way: *to abuse a horse; to abuse one's eyesight.*

to speak insultingly, harshly, and unjustly to or about; revile; malign.

to commit sexual assault upon.

Obsolete. to deceive or mislead.

In today's world there are many types of abuse, alcohol, drug, Physical Abuse, Sexual Abuse, Emotional or Psychological Abuse, Neglect, Abandonment, Financial or Material Exploitation, Self-neglect and the list goes on and on. Each one is different in its own right and some of these abuses affect everyone in your family, loved ones and friends which some abuses affect only you mentality.

I am not saying that mine is the worst but something that I feel is not known to others in the world, which people should be aware of and there is another type of abuse out there that people have very little knowledge of or even been studied.

Being a mistake to me is up there as second or even third type of abuse that is a painful type of abuse a child should not have to go thru, you feel unwanted, unloved and even not part of a family.

As you read this book which is the first time every writing one and which is very difficult for someone with learning disabilities. I have told the editors to leave the book as I have written it using words that sound the same but spelled different and that have two meanings, run on sentences and even miss spelling,(but thank you Microsoft word for spell check wish I had that going thru high school and college). These are just part of the problems I faced growing up and still now.

To this day I still read at a 8th grade level and spell at a 6th grade level. This makes working at a corporate level very hard and sometimes embarrassing but I feel this issue makes my work ethic very focused so I do not make mistakes double and triple check my work and as we go along in this book I will show you how my do not give up attitude and I will not fail has set me apart and above of some people that are straight A students.

There was US study done in 2009 and it said that all children from kindergarten to college grads that there is 13% of all students that have some king of Learning disabilities, and these disabilities are not well known to anyone in the late 50's early 60's.

Schools just felt you were some kind of behavior disorder child having trouble getting along with other students and how to sit and listen in class with out disturbing others.

But having trouble understanding how to spell and read simple words was my issue and there were deeper problems no one knew or understood about me. This will be covered as I explain why I wanted to write this book and to other parents and understand you should not ignore your child having problems in school or push it off on the school system let them do it.

A child needs there parents to set the example for the child and step forward to nurture there child and be understanding plus even look for ways to encourage the child to find out what they like to learn about and use that as a tool or a stepping stone to over come a learning disabilities.

There are many ways to help a child or young adult to help them read better and to help improve their spelling, one thing I found out was and I know I will cover this deeper in this book, find what interest your child what they want to learn about and then get this type of reading material for them.

Let me tell you this is a big step to improve reading habits, for me I love reading about planets and how they are formed plus how earth quakes happen and plate tectonics. I can read a book from cover to cover when it comes to what interest me.

But you will see how my life evolved and the issues and problems I faced as being labeled a mistake and being abused as one, every day as I grew up going thru school, college, work and relationships what I did to over come my problems and the many mistakes I made in life with work, relationships and in general, which there are some of these painful memories I still have to deal and live with and what I struggle with now in my day to day life.

Not all have been painful there has been many success and positive things that has happen, I know it is because I work very hard to be success full in life and when you get knocked down you need get back up stronger and better, because when it comes right down too it you have no one but yourself to rely on you are your own cheerleader, support system and your own inner parent.

But when talking about your own inner parent what I mean by that is you need to love your self, be happy with how you are and what can you do to improve who you are and care for yourself. If others took this approach the world would become a better place, we could look at life and say what I can do to be better for myself and be better to people around me.

In the dedication I talked about promised myself that would be a better father to my sons then my dad was I am not saying my father was a bad father but I wanted to be a better one then he was, plus be able teach my sons what my father have taught me about life, in some respects I am better then my father and in others words I feel I have failed them. This is very hard to admit to ones self you feel you have failed being a good father but I know there are things in there life growing up I could have been better at and was not.

But the good in all this was I did not totally fail them I am not perfect and I never calm to be perfect please do not misunderstand me I did more with my sons and been there for them when they really needed me then my father did.

My sons and I did many things together as father and sons which I have cherished and will always have these memories. As a father you need to keep an open line of communication with your children let them know they can come to you with any problem and that you will be there for them, and help them thru the problem.

Most of all let your children know when they have a problem that you will listen and be a good listener and open your heart to them no matter what let then know you will never ever yell at them insult them or even mentally abuse them for the problem or anything they did that's your child that wants to talk you.

The reason I am talking about this is I did not have that kind of parent that as a child I could go to, my father was the old world Italian, a child should be seen and not heard but he had a soft spot for me. I could tell him almost anything (remember I said almost anything) there were things I did not want to tell father because he would of killed me.

He was a very good listener but that was about it he would not have much to say but when he did he spoke volumes.

On the other hand a son needs to be able to talk to his mother to on different issues but this person I could not talk to with out fear of being emasculated, insulted, or even yelled at, I will cover more of this as we move on in this book.

The point I am making is your children look up to you as a role model, or mentor and if you break that where do they go for love and understanding you children my go outside the home. If your children go outside the home to find that understanding and love then you have lost them and it can be forever if you do not have that open line of communication. Yes I know as your children grow up and become young adults they have close friends that they will confide in share there thoughts, problems and some of their most intimate secrets.

But as parents we need to be there for the most important ones and mothers you are the ones the will be the most important ones in your child's life, you have to be the most nurturing and loving when you child comes to you with any problem and all problems.

To much today our children are out fending for themselves and they get in with the wrong crowds get into bigger trouble and problems, which all could have been avoided if as parents we were there for them. This has been said and I will say it again our children get into trouble or turn bad because we as parents were not there for our children.

Sorry if I offend some people but it is true our children get into trouble or join gangs because they want to belong, as parents we need to make our children belong to your family and it start with you and it starts at home.

My apology for being on the soap box lecturing but I want to prove a point I did not have very open parents to communicate with, I do give credit to my father who keep me on the straight and narrow. Also were some words I will never forget as long as I live that my father said to me that keep me out of trouble, he said you do something wrong and get arrested do not call me. If that does not keep you on the right path what does, yes that sound harsh but in those days it worked.

There were other one sentence direction my father was good at but that was him and not me I am a little different dad. He taught me one thing that I am still grateful for, he said if you want something go out and get a job and work for what you want because no one is going to hand it to you. This will give you no greater pleasure in life working hard for something and owning it.

There has been many examples were working hard for something and buying it yourself is a big deal especially when you purchase your very first car this was a long process I looked a new ones and used ones. This process if I remember took about a couple of weeks before deciding on a car that I wanted.

Of course never go car shopping with your mother and defiantly not with my mother not only did she try to tell me what kind of car to get but what color too.

Besides owning not just a home but the wife and I work very hard all our lives and have what we have today, we own a vacation home plus a rental home.

I know others have the same and more but, not bad for someone with learning disabilities that never made a lot of money in his life raised two children put one thru college and the other did his own college credits thru this job.

This is were you will start to understand who I am and were I came from being respect oneself and where others gave up on you especially one of your parents labeled a mistake, how you do not give up on your goals, dreams and yourself, love and.

Somehow I did not know the magnitude if this issue until I met young lady that was running for Library trustee to replace some members that left and I was on the board already for year as we got to know each other over 2 years she became like a sister to me and I could see she was hiding something I just could not put a finger on it but it was apparent we had something in common.

One night the wife and I were at dinner that her house and we met her husband we were having a nice time and the discussion came to our parents and then I started talking about how my mother was to me and how she labeled me a mistake then I began to tell her about some of the abuse I had gone thru and all the stuff I went thru in my life.

For some reason I felt I could tell her about my history and knew she would understand of course she was shocked to hear that and we had the same thing in common and she was also abused as a child and even to this day what she goes thru, so one day she sent me a letter that she had written her parents just recently and I want to share this with you to validate some of my story and it sounds the same as her story of abuse.

An Open Letter to My Father and Mother:

Or should I refer to you as "Daddy Dearest" and "Mommy Dearest"??? Not that you would understand that, but to me it makes perfect sense. Why an open letter? Because. That is all you need to know. I do not owe you an explanation nor do I owe justification to this because. I woke up this morning with hate in my heart. I woke up this morning with no love in my heart – and no love in my again broken heart which struggles to love you with the little pieces that you leave behind in your verbal warfare. I hate to love you and I love to hate you. It is so much easier for me to hate you because hate is just that – malice, dislike, detest and resentment for something and that something is you. If you don't know, I really struggle with loving you and I struggle because you make it impossible for me to love you after repeatedly breaking my heart into little pieces. I struggle with this love that I have for you because I don't feel loved or appreciated but more along the lines of stupid and unworthy. I walk on eggshells with you because you constantly judge me and you are not an entity or God or worthy of doing this. In fact, I don't believe you are worthy of a daughter such as me. But you know what, I can't hate. Sure, I can talk about it and scream it out at the top of my lungs but that again is just talk. I can't hate you because it's not going to make me a better person and my God, I want to be the best person I can possibly be because you are very ignorant of the fact that I possess many positive traits – one of them being compassion, sincerity, honesty, integrity, wit, love and most of all humility. Unlike you, I am keenly aware of how I treat people. Unlike you, I have compassion for other human beings. Unlike you, I still struggle with judging people, but I try very hard not to do this. I try to show a love for other humans but most of all, I bite my tongue – something which you still remain clueless about. I also walk on eggshells with you because I have to watch what I say and what I tell you I'm doing – because you still do not accept me for the person that I am and that alone hurts me more than I can expound on in a simple letter. Children look to their parents for approval and when they don't get that approval, they question themselves. They also have problems with self-esteem and confidence and thanks to both of you; I have a problem with these things – thanks for the lifelong gift of a lack of self-esteem and confidence. Honestly, I don't know why you adopted me – because you wanted to impress your friends?? Or did you really want a child? I doubt it was the second because I have yet to feel those wants. Today I will struggle with many different emotions. I will cry and I will cuss your name today. But that is only today. Luckily I am a survivor and survive I will – maybe with a little help from people who know how to treat others – my friends. I always said that if your friends treated you the way your family did, they would never be your friends. Well guess what, I have some very close friends who have treated me better than you ever have. Today if I was to meet you in heaven, I would walk away. I truly think the only peace I will ever have in my life is when I am dead but maybe not even then because God probably looked favorably on both of you and I will forever spend the rest of my days again in your despicable and despised presence. I cannot say this enough today – I hate you dad and I hate you mom. I hate that you are so wishy-washy and not definitive, I hate that you know nothing of love and most of all I hate you because you have no clue whatsoever of how to treat a child or the lasting emotional effects you leave on a child when they become an adult. What is even sadder is that it is that much harder for me to love my husband when I cannot even love myself – how do I explain that one? You have hurt me beyond comprehension and beyond what my heart can contain anymore. You have hurt me in the deepest and most profound ways, ways in which I cannot even explain anymore and am tired of crying about to try and explain. YOU DON'T DESERVE ME and YOU DON'T DESERVE MY LOVE!!!!! The only thing you deserve is to be left in solitude so you cannot hurt anyone anymore ever again! You can both go to hell because I hope I never see you in heaven!

Signed
S G.

What she write is very compelling and pain full to read I know her pain and I feel her pain we sometime talk about it and help each other thru are pain but you never really get over the pain there are scars that are too deep.

You can cover up your feelings with laughter or silly behavior which is something I do all the time, to hide the hurt deep inside were you hope it will not come out and surface but something always brings it up and you feel the pain and the felling that you have been missing something in your life, so this is way I am writing this book kind of like her letter express my feelings and maybe get over the pain "I hope".

But I know I will not just hide it and try to lock it away but watching TV and seeing the support and love that other parents give their children and watching the love that they express for them is overwhelming something I will never know something I have never felt.

Having that warm embrace of a mother telling me how proud she is of me and how much she will support whatever I do in life and encourage me to go after my dream or a goal and help you up when you fall.

Plus being there from me to have someone to talk to and confide in someone to tell your securities too or ask advice about a subject. That is why I need to get my message out to all parents to stop this abuse and try to make you better parents.

Watching other parents stand behind their children and giving support must be such a great feeling inside of love, I do not know what that fells like when I stand I stand and have stood alone which is such a hollow feeling inside that is why I use a spiritual person to fill my void and it helps me to be a better person to my family and others.

Chapter 2

Being born in 1953 "which gives my age way" I was the second born my sister is the oldest by two years, but we need to have a starting point, and it started in Chicago not sure were to this day? But we did not stay long we moved to Suburban town just outside of Chicago were my story and reason for this book started.

My father bough a two flat home with an apartment on the second floor that he rented out which help paid for his mortgage, as I said my father was good at what he did and taught me well.

I can remember of having a normal childhood from the photos and memories I have of me and my sister, photos of birthday party's with family and friends everything looks as a normal loving family should.

My father for all his working career was a factory worker always working long hours coming home late mother stayed home to raised us until both me and my sister were old enough to start Catholic school. Mother was not much of a stay at home mom so she stated me early into kindergarten which is were I feel some of my learning disabilities developed and let me tell you in the late 50's early 60's Catholic school was not known for higher education, but discipline and respect is what was the most important subject taught along with the understanding of God and your religion.

As a very young child going to school I had trouble focusing in class not because I had a behavior disorder but I was developing very bad allergies as I went into first grade that started in the early spring and lasted till the first frost of winter this would affect my eyes and they would itch burn and tear with pus and a runny nose constantly all day long.

I had trouble seeing the board and understand what was going on in class with this constant rubbing of the eyes that were burning, red and watering, by the end of the day my shirt was a mess, my mother did not understand what I was trying to tell her when I tried telling her what was going on all day she would just yell and scream at me to stop wiping my noise on my shirt and give me tissues so I would stop messing up my school shirt!

My mother could only understand one thing and that was being a problem child causing problems getting bad grades and not listing in class or to the Nuns.

I took my father just too look at me a till mother there is something wrong with our son and we should get him to a doctor. This took several trips to different doctors until one doctor took one look at me and told my parents you son has allergies and the only thing the doctor could do is give a prescription for ointment and put in my eyes. This process took at least 15 minutes in the morning but would not last all day.

By then the damage was done being set back in simple reading spelling and phonics made learning difficult, knowing to this day I had a learning disability just amplified my problem in trying to catch up in school to understand was impossible and I fell further and further behind, plus as a child trying to reach out and express ones frustration parents back then even old world Italians like mine were children should be seen and not heard. All I could do was suppress my feelings and deal with the rejections and the failure.

My mother was not a very understanding or well educated person her self and trying to help me read and spell at home was not her strong point.

It felt as if I was bothering her and she had other things to do.

Father got a better job but had to work the grave yard shift and was never home as regular fathers were so not have him home to help with my studies that really left my mother alone and me study by myself.

As I struggled with my studies in second and third grade and turned for my mother for help I could see and feel the resentment growing not a lot at first but more as I got older.

Mother did not have the patience or the ability to help teach a child how to read or spell, just yelling and screaming at me because I was having trouble.

By the end of the third grade we move from one town to another and my father had a custom home built and were we started public schools. Where I soon found myself trying to read and write at a 4th grade level which I was not even close to keeping up.

As I tried to keep up in class my allergies we not helping and my ability to learn was being hampered by my allergies to the point I was going to summer school to catch up but this was not fixing the problem because the schools could not see I had a learning disability.

One day in class the teacher was giving instructions on our assignments for the next day and of course my allergies were flaring up and I was rubbing my eyes and wiping off the tears from the burning and itching of course the teacher saw this and knew I was not leasing and asked me a question and of course I did not hear it. Her questions was do you want a dunce sign to wear the rest of the day and I said sure not know what she asked me? So she walks over and puts this sign around my neck saying I am a dunce.

I am having trouble in school as it is and this just made it worse this was just killing me and being ridiculed by my class mates and of course not letting me forget it for the rest of the year and which followed to even to the next year.

Coming home and trying to study and reading out loud to my mother was not easy, every miss pronounced word or fumbling over words as I read became more and more of a chore because of the yelling and screaming at me with name calling of "what are you stupid you can not do anything you will not become anything in life, how you going to get a job if you can not read and spell."

Going thru this at an early age you loose all self esteem and confidence, other children would see this and then I would be made fun of and bullied to the point I stayed away from other kids and had very little to no friends and to the point every one though I was shy as I went into the 5th grade.

Summer school and tutoring continued I would make some progress away from home but having to study in a not caring abusive environment were your own mother could not help or even try to be understanding with love made reading and spelling impossible. To even this day I have trouble spelling or reading out loud in front of people, coworkers, friends and family. If someone is standing over my shoulder I find myself not able to spell simple words and even read, I know this comes from mother standing over me and yelling in my ear and being terrified of making the smallest mistake.

By this time going into the 6th grade mother was that her wits end and left it up to the schools to fix my problem and she just worried about cleaning the house and going to work. Entering the 6th grade even in a new school I was labeled as a problem and stupid student. Stating my day in 6th grade when the class would start grammar and spelling I would have to leave my class and go to the second grade and start learning how to spell and read all over again. But showing the second grade class teacher that is was better then second grade and she had me moved to the third grade for grammar and spelling.

Still how humiliating to a child this was and this did not take my classmates long to find out were was I going and we all know how that goes in school being made fun of with more embarrassment adding insult to injury. Going home with this on my mind there was no mother to get help love and understating; dad was at work doing his grave yard shift.

But all was not totally bad in 6th grade I had a very good teacher who started noticing I was not stupid. Even in 6th grade she was told to dumb it down for me when math time came I was given 4th grade math to do were my classmates were doing decimal math division and multiplying, I was given easy plus and minuses math exercises.

One day I ask my teacher I can do decimals let me show you I can do the same work everyone else is doing, the look on my teachers face was priceless! Reluctantly she gave it to me and I proceed to do the exercises and Aced the work. At that point for math I was treated the rest of my classmates but still had to go into the third grade for the rest of the year for reading and spelling.

Over summer break going to summer school for more help in learning grammar and reading there were times I would go by the park and watch other kids try out for little league. (Back then you did not join little league you tried out to make the team.) I was watching the try outs and seeing some of my 6th grade class mates trying out, so I went home and got my glove and when back to the field to ask can it try out. So the coach said take the field with the other guys and I will hit some fly balls so I can see how you can do. Well seeing this by my class mates I was getting heckled from them you know are too dumb to read to dumb to play baseball.

Nothing pleased me more then showing them I could play with the best of them and of course catching a pop fly was oh the dummy gets the easy ones to catch, and the of course the coach could not hear this as you are out in the outfield.

By the end of the practice the coach said to me you play well enough to make the team, were is your mom or dad I said they both work and cannot be here, then the coach said you need to have a parent here to sign you up and bring you to the games you cannot join without one of them.

Will there is nothing left to say my father could not be there since he started working day time hours and over time he was not around too much on Saturdays and mother was to busy cleaning house and getting ready for work I guess playing base ball was out of the question.

I did go home and asked dad can you sign me up, of course taking time out and as I said he worked a lot of Saturdays taking me to games was out of the question, and mother home in the morning could do it but no! She had no confidence in me to do good in school how could I play baseball. It was you know so in so son got hurt playing base ball you do not need to play you're not that good and besides you are not good in school you need to buckle down at getting better grads before you can play baseball so forget it.

Now this word buckle down is word I cannot stand hearing to this day it makes me sick just hearing this word because this is all I heard growing up I never used this word around my sons NEVER used it.

A child needs the support of there parents to push you a little and give you confidence help up believe in yourself and work with you to develop who you are and what you are going to be.

As a father myself I always believed in my sons and when they wanted to try something I helped all I could and praised them when they did well and even when they failed I was there to support them and give them encouragement to do better. That is way today my sons are successful and they can do anything they put there mind to it.

I made it a point to be were every my sons were when they tried to do something in a play, sports, cooking contest, graduating or what ever I was there for them.

Sorry that I got off track but I wanted to point out some of the abuse I was putting up with as a child that lead me to write this book, so let's get back to how my progressing in school kept going and were I became self efficient to make it thru school.

After moving into the 7th grade I was put in a behavior disordered classes which looking back on this now these other 7th graders looked like killers and thugs. I did not have these problem just learning disabilities which no one cared about in the school system back then a child with this issue you were dismissed as a problem child.

Even my parents did not care dad was now to busy working regular hours on the day shift no time to come into school and talk to the teachers and of course mother could care less would not dare to miss her shift going to work as a wateriest and take an interest in her child struggling in school. The only time mother took interest is when the school would call and told her what they were going to try next to help me, all she did was say that sounds good let's try that.

Half way thru the year the program for the behavior disorder call was broken up and we all moved into regular classes and of course more embarrassment. 8th grad was more of the same and could not wait to graduate out of junior high and start into high school were I though I could start over and no one would know my pass history, well silly me no chance of that.

I again want to jump off the track as point out some personal achievement here in 8th grade, because the abuse of not having a parent supporting you as a child being labels a mistake you look for support else were and sometimes in my case you find a little bit, in some cases earn some respect at the same time.

In 8th grade we had touch foot ball games in gym class and as always I was picked last for a team and the game was played around me were I was not part of the team. I was put as a wide receiver away from the plays and the real game, until one game we were behind and need to make a touchdown to win and placed as a wide receiver I know I could not do anything to help. As the play stated and no one covered me because the other team did not think I could even catch the football I ran to the coroner of the end zone all by my self I turned around and found the ball coming my way all I did was reach up grab it we won!

From that point one our quarter back started throwing me the ball more and more still some of my class mates did not believe I could do anything as good as they could. So all I could do is to prove I was just as good as they were, another game out as wide receiver one of my lustrous bullies was covering me and he was told to watch me of course he did not. The play started and I went up the field wide open our quarter back laid it out for me to catch and run it into the end zone.

Some times the bullies do not always win all the time and it was a good felling to be trusted and supported by others on a team and here you build confidence with them and yourself. I think this is where I stated developing my own self worth and confidence knowing I could do anything myself as long as I put my mind to it.

Ok back to the process of starting high school was no different then any other school I was just a little luckier cause it was such a big school and I got a little lost in the shuffle, my learning disabilities still followed me I was put in all the basic courses like basic math, English, science and history. Plus your same class mates following you and of course letting even one else know your history.

But there I stated meeting new students making new friends who did not care about my history or back ground and I stated developing my own personality and who I was I climbed out of my shell, my mother always said that my best friend Ken got me out of my shell of shyness which is not true at all it is just a way for mother to try and control me and make me feel less of a person.

Getting out of my shell was a process I did by myself I looked at myself in the mirror one day and told myself you are not going to be shy anymore you will be outgoing and fun to be around.

Of course not in school because some people would not understand the new me and I know I would be made more fun of so it was outside of school I was my new self with a little more confidence and less shyness. My grades improved a little too about a C to a C+ average in high school as I worked harder and harder on my disability by myself of course mother only worried about it when the report cards came out but as long as I was passing classes she didn't care, mother did not need to get involved or had to worry about me and my problems in school just clean the house and go to work.

As a young man growing up there was a new problem facing me "Girls" of course not having a mother to go to and ask questions about them it was tuff to interact with girls understand them and talk or even to be a friend specialty in high school were you really started to socialize more with other students?

As time when on I started to learn the hard way on how to talk to girls, making mistakes and learning from them most of all how to treat them with kindness and respect. Dating was another hole set of issues from me and my shyness it continued around girls this was even harder when it came to talking to them and not having a good mother figurer to look up to and talk to, I really felt to this day that some of the failed relationships I had with some of the girls I dated were because of my own relationship with my mother.

I was a junior in high school when I really started dating but my best friend Ken set me up on a blind date with this girl that his girl friend knew and it was I guess my first introduction on how to get to understand them which was very difficult for me not knowing how to interact with them.

After meeting this girl we kind of hit it off for the most part because remember I did not understand girls and she asked me to the turnabout dance which I replayed "I will let you know want to see if something better comes along".

Really I said that are you kidding what kind of IDIOT am I where do I get off saying that to a girl asking me out!!! As I said I had a lot to learn about talking to girls. My friend came up to me and said what did you say to her you were waiting for something better are you nuts!! Yes I said I am sorry I have no idea where that came from. I apologized for that but we did go to the dance.

A few months later prom was coming up which I had no plans on going because I was to shy or scared to talk to girls (No I was not going to ask another girl to prom because I had a girl friend I am not that much of an Idiot) I asked her to prom and we double dated with my best friend Ken and his girl.

Before the end of our junior year we broke up she was getting I felt serous and I was not prepared to handle that kind of relationship so we did not last long, I did not know what to do or were to go. I talked about this with my best friend but he was having his own problems with his girl friend so I just let it slip away, why because I did not what to do or were to go not knowing how to treat them or how to get along or even to express my own feelings is were I failed and that is something I did not like doing failing at something even in relationships. They say girls mature faster then boys and I know that is right I was not mature enough to handle that!

I know some or most of my issues with girls were with my own issues with my mother. Were would I go to ask question or even advise so one night I got a call from a girl and all I got was from mother was "Oh I guess it is time to tell you about the birds and the bee's" (yes she was trying to be funny) which she had no idea how to be funny, "no mother I said we learned that in school I know all about that stuff"! (Nice help HU).

Not knowing what to say and how to say it along with handle certain situations and when to say I am sorry or what is the right thing to say. Really ruined relations with girls, as I think back about it now, there were a few girls I know I really hurt over my years of dating and doing it wrong so to that I say to all those girls I hurt I am truly sorry.

Father was not much help either who had is own problems with mother, dad was just someone I could go to and borrow his car for going out on dates. Dads own relationship with mother was not one you could easily talk about, but that is for another time or another book?

In December after I turned 16 my dad bough me my first set golf dad clubs for Christmas and in the spring of that year he started teaching me all about golf and thru summer how to play golf and surprisingly I picked the game up fast and was starting to get pretty good at the game.

Moving into my senor year was more of a break out year for me personally I was developing more confidence and more of my own personality (the new me) and of course all the older kids moving out of school and not being there to bully me was better. Of course I still had my other class mates who were there to still bully me and push me around but as I said before our high school was big and I got lost in the crowed and most of the other class mates were busy with baseball, football and other activities I was low on there radar.

As a senior I tried out for the senior golf team as you know I got my golf set as a sophomore two years before and was working on my game all that time.

Of course from some of my class mates getting wind of me joining the golf team and of course I was catching a lot of flack over that, but my new found confidence was fuelling by my ability to play golf really helped in every qualifying match that I played and my game was good and kept making the cut and getting closer to making the team, until the last round of qualifying I played one of my worst rounds of golf and did not make the team.

On that day I learn that in your life you will fail and fall down again and again but you get up more and more determined not to give up and never quite. I know this is were I got my first taste of my own determination and the

I will not quite attitude that makes me what I am today and that anytime there is a challenged and someone say that cannot be done I will be the one that will take that challenged and succeed.

But of course I could tell dad was prod of me for trying and we worked more on my golf game more and more together, father and I bonded more and we really had fun together.

I can remember even to this day when dad and I played golf together I would hit my drive about 50 yards head of dad's drive but I was off to the right and is drive was in the middle of the fairway he would take out is 3 wood and hit it right up the middle to were he had a short chip and one put for par.

Me on the other hand I hit my second shot in the bunker then across the green to the other bunker get on the green and three put for a 7 and I can see his face as if it was right in front of me and his words ring in my head as he would say what the heck are you doing!!! You can play better than this what have I we worked on you need to keep that in focus.

I have learned more from my father on the golf course and about life with him then anything person that a child could lean in a life time. I miss him very much even to this day but when I am on the golf course I know he is with me and when I have a bad hole I hear him say "What the heck our you doing" God rest this sole!

After my senior year my father offered to send me to golf school but my real love for the game was not there yet so I turned him down I did not want to give up my summers to date and be with my friends (ok here you go opportunity missed we lean by our mistakes) so later my father asked me again and of course I said no (how dumb was I miss opportunities twice and to this day I am still kicking myself over this because I love the game of golf so much). I know my own lace of self confidence played a big role in me turning father down in going to golf school.

Because of my father teaching me the game of golf, I learned golf it is like life you have good rounds and you have bad rounds and this game is very humbling just like life. Golf is self improving sport and you play the game by your self and you depend on one else but yourself even thou you compete agents someone else it is up to you if you win or lose there is not team to depend on just yourself just like life.

I really thank my father for teaching me this game of golf I believe it help me in life to understand what life is, and life is not fare or easy but you never give up or let it beat you, it will knock you down but you need to get up and lean from your mistakes.

I worked very hard on my grades still they were averaging around the C to C+ range, but I was felling good about my learning disability I felt that I had it beat, little did I know when I want to college it was time to wake up and see the reality in life. (I will get in to more of that later).

Getting into my senor year I was looking forward to graduating and getting into college and starting my carrier (of what was going to be I did not know yet) I did not have much help from my parents for one thing I did not what to work in a factory like my father because I know the hours were long and hard and father he put in a lot of hours all his life and I did not want to follow my mother in the restaurant industry so I was getting into business management classes in my finial year of high school.

My struggles with girls and dating still continued even after I left high school and it followed me in to college.

I got a job in the local grocery store that mother helped me get so I would not be sitting around the house all summer with nothing to do. But working is a great way to learn about business and watching how my boss managed people and learn my managing skills thru others, but after a year I left that job and took another job in a bank and of all things a stock boy. Yes a stock boy! And no I was not stocking money in the vault as I was teased by my friends and of course mother.

Working at the bank I meet this young girl that was working in the accounting department who instantly cough my eye she could see that I was very shy and would start talking to me first. I started asking the other ladies in the accounting department about her which they immediately know I liked her and they told me she like me. I found out she was a sophomore in my high school but with different time shifts at school we never saw each other because I was a senior.

As time went on I let my guard down and some of my shyness were I started to get to know her and she got to know me, we started dating and since she was 17 her father said she had to be home by 10:30pm which I respected his demand and followed to the minute.

She went to my senior prom and again doubled with my best friend and his girlfriend and after graduation we still dated thru her junior year and I went to her junior prom and I was in my first year of my junior college and I think I was the only guy there at her prom that was a college student. Our relationship flourished and of course fell for her like a ton of bricks, but as always young love does not last and good things do come to an end.

We had our issues and one of the biggest issues was religion and she used this reason to break up with me it was something about me being a catholic I was not christen for whatever reason she used to break it off. Later I learned she was scared of our relationship and I was moving too fast for her, but all she had to do was tell me and I would have backed off.

But I have learned also in life that things happen for a reason and something's happen that is out of our control and no madder what we do nothing will change it and that is what we have to live with.

But of course this ripped my heart out and sent be back into my shell and not wanting to open up my heart again, with not having a mother to go to and console I just had my best friend and his girl friend to talk to, not easy for a young man needing his mother and not having one is very though to handle.

I left the bank shortly after that because she was still working there and I could not handle seeing her all the time and not talking to me. I promised myself that I would not let this ever happen to me again. "Yah Right what was I thinking" Starting to look for a new job that would suit my hours at college my dad showed me an ad for a department stores looking for help some of you may know them as Venture.

At an early age I started to learn there were better jobs out there that I could get without my mother not get for me. In that time you could find a better job making more money.

Still my parents could not afford or would not pay to sending me away to college I knew I could not go away to some universities because of my grade point average being so low.

So I started to look for a college close to home where I could commute. That was harder than it sounds some colleges would not take me because of my grade point average and the ones that would accept me they were too expensive for me.

So I went to a junior college in Illinois which I could afford and at the time it cost me $25 a credit hour and full time student was 14 or more credit hours a semester and then all I had to pay for were books, which I could handle.

Here I thought all I needed was to get better grades after two years then I could move into a 4 year college and finish my degree in business management.

Well not at a retail department store but I went in applied for the job and got the position of sales assistant a glorified name for "stock boy" and the job paid minimum wage of $1.90 per hour big money back then, plus trying to save money for college, dating, and going out with my friends was tuff. I put in a lot of hours in to make enough money to do all the things I wanted to do. Well burn the candle at both ends was not the smartest thing I ever did working long hours going to college and dating I had very little time for studies and sleep!

With this work and school schedule the only thing that paid for this was my grades, I was barely keeping them above "C" and if I wanted to move into a 4 year college these grads had to be at least a "B" average. But I was able to graduate from junior college and I found a 4 year college that would accept me with my grade point average but when I started my first semester I was instantly put on probation.

Staying out of probation and not getting kick out of college was very hard to do, every time I told my department manager I needed to work less and go to school more he would reduce my hours to 16 a week next week they would go up to 20 then 24 then 32 hours.

The department manager keep relying on me and needed to keep the department up and looking good, I guess I should of taken that as a complement that I was doing such a good job the manager and he depended on me to take care of the department.

I started to insert myself in this job learning how to be a good employee and working hard (which I learned from my father) as I realize being a good employee I was getting good reviews and praise, something I never got from my mother.

My manager began to depend on me to take care of things when he we off or when the store was busy and he needed someone over a big sale weekend and again my hours became a lot to take while I was going to college. You learn a lot about yourself when working almost full time and going to college full time this will build character and develop a very good working habit. It feels as if you are working to earn something weather self respect and accomplishment of a goal. Learning how to work hard for something and earn it.

I know the job I have today is because I worked my way true college during my interview the VP of operations asked were I went to college and I paid my own way by working, his said good for you and I knew at that time he was impressed with me and I got the job. Ok back to what I was talking about.

Praise was something I loved and as I said below I could not get enough of the word "praise".

So the definition of this word expresses warm approval or admiration of.

Commend, express admiration for, applaud, pay tribute to, speak highly of, eulogize, compliment, congratulate, sing the praises of, rave about, go into raptures about, heap praise on, wax lyrical about, make much of, pat on the back, take one's hat off to, lionize, admire, hail, ballyhoo;

This was like a drug to me every time I get praise my heart fell like the love of my life told me she loved me for the first time, and I wanted more and more of that word praise, to the point I would do anything for it.

I would work extra days or overtime head up inventory or do special projects at work or work over night in a locked down store to rest a department for a season change just for good job Shawn or you did a nice work just so I would get some kind of praise.

Even to this day I still want hear praise and I work very hard to get it I am obsessed with this word and want to get praise I think it makes me go above and beyond what normal people do in their jobs.

Today I am a purchasing manager for a large manufacture and production relies on me to make sure material is in stock and on time and on time for production, also taking care of maintenance needs to make sure our machines are running at top performance and keep spare parts on hand for repair and for minimum down time that can cost a company big money.

I take my job very seriously looking for ways to save money and keep our company running and making money I work very hard doing this in hopes to here and get a little bit of praise that is why I do what I do in my day to day life just for the word of "PRAISE".

That is way today I give my son's praise when and were ever I can they should feel good about themselves it builds confidence and a very strong person.

So parents please give your children praise on everything they do, no matter how small it is to the biggest accomplishment in there life you will see the transformation right before your eyes and if you have a child with learning disabilities this little word will go a long way to help them do better.

So going back to working at the department store there were many opportunity for me to meet of all thing girls, which is what I did start to dated, at first I started with one and meet another girl so I dated her too at the same time then on to 3 girls I dated as many different girls as I could. Break up with one find another there was a time that I was dating as many as 5 girls at one time our head casher called it my harem.

Yes I said 5 at a time and no I am not exaggerating of course dating this many girls were killing my studies and my bank account but I did not care.

And NO! I was not trying to be some kind of jerk by dating so many and not being true to just one girl, this was one of the ways not letting anyone girl get close to me again because I did not what to get hurt anymore.

But still not let anyone girl get close to me was very hard because I wanted to be loved just like any child wanting to be loved by their parents.

I craved that love and by dating I was getting some of that affection that was absent in my life and looking for everywhere but committing to just one person was impossible for me to do so because I did not have it in my life and I did not know how to express it then and even to this day I have a very hard time expressing my love to other people that I love so much. So when it comes to dating girls that was easy but committing is very hard as I explain more.

As I said I did not what to get close to any girl but there is always an exception to the rule as I let another girl get close to me again, but she found out I was dating others and not just her and she was so upset she broke up with me "serves me right you know"!

But I had to slow it down because my grades were not getting any better and not getting enough sleep made it tuff to stay awake in class.

So I will finish my dating issues in my second year at this junior college I was taking a speech class (not easy for a student with learning disabilities) because I was thinking

39

of a carrier as a radio announcer this would force me to read better and not be shy in front of people.

I even took a class call radio and TV announcing were we all did our own radio and TV shows this class was so much fun I learned a lot about myself how to work with other and lead people. The teacher that was teaching this class was a very aggressive type he had us doing so many different parts of radio and TV from in front of the camera to behind the seines directing and producing our own shows.

One class the teacher asked us if we wanted to televise the schools basketball games with me as the announcer and a crew for cameras with a director and producer we all jumped at this opportunity and that weekend we televised our first collect basketball game.

It was as little ruff for the first few minuets of the game for me a little nervous and could not get started on calling the game right but our color man jumped in and took over till I was more confident and use to calling the game before we were done with the first televising of the game we all were pros at it.

So the recorded game was played the next day in the school cafeteria and there was a crowed around the TV leasing to our telecast of the game and our teacher said we were a hit and we could televise ever home game which went well for a few months until someone damaged some of the camera equipment and we were blamed for it and our short lived TV queries were gone, but this was such good experience it kind of guided me into another path and away from announcing.

As you would guess I meet another girl in my speech class who I let get to close to me, (this was not smart, not smart at all) she was beautiful and she was everything I wanted in a girl friend, and what did this girl see in me I do not know?? But of course my inability to communicate, to be understand, and shearing my feelings was my own demise.

We could not be dating 4 months and we were close very close I was having strong feelings for her but could not express them to her and did not know how or let my heart say how I felt. So one night we were sitting in her house alone watching TV and she said those words, I am falling in love with you!! When she said that it felt as if someone put a electrical charge to my heart and it shot thru my whole body like nothing I ever felt before, but (dang-it) I could not open my mouth and say it back I wanted to say it but the words would not come out of my mouth.

I did not know what to say I was in (shock and aw) you could say but she knew what happened with my history of one girl friend in high school and understood it and knew it was hard from me to say the same thing back and gave me a break and some time.

But I also did not let her know of my past and why I was having relationship issues with girls and why I could not communicate, and to be understand, even shearing my feelings with her.

Maybe just maybe things would have been different if I could have said the right things. Well we lasted almost another year as I found a local college that would except me for my grade point average, were we would still date and be close to each other.

But the relationship did not last I was still having problems with being understanding and sensitive to her and our problems.

I could not commit to her and I was breaking promises, one night she wanted to see a play at her old high school and wanted to go and see some of her old friends, but of course I HATE PLAYS I said no do not want to go but gave in to her requests we went to the play but I sat there like a spoiled 3 year old not wanting to eat his vegetables I bet the look on my face was the face of a spoiled child.

As time when on in our relationship I would turn to me friends for advise they tried to tell me I was nuts for acting like this and should let my guard down and tell her how much I cared for her. But did not listen very well maybe if I had a mother I could talk to and confide in and she was an understanding mother things may have turned out differently.

But no I had no one to turn to so one night our announcing class went out to a restaurant for a few beers and as you would of guessed I meet a girl and we started talking about different things and some how we got on the subject of my girl friend and our issues (or my issue) and found out she was having the same problem with her boy friend.

We decided to meet again and get into our subject more and hopped we could help each other out with our boy friend and girl friend issues. This went on for a few weeks and I felt we were making progress on helping each other out. Yes you think I was cheating on my girl friend with this other girl but I was not we never held hands or even kissed just talked and were friends.

As you would of guessed I was out with my girl friend and we having our problems talking I took her home after our date and some how I blurted out I was talking to another girl about us and she took it as I was seeing another girl she left my car crying and I never saw her again.

This had to be the worst night of my life I thru away this wonderful person because I could not figure out how to have a relationship with and girl. Well maybe if I had a real mother I could go to and talk about my problems openly and not get emasculated and insulted maybe things could have been different.

But when you love someone you do things for them and you should just do it wit out question and this took me a very long time for me to get it and understand it but the damage was done, this brake up was one of the hardest one's I had to go thru and to deal with another one to recover from because of how much I cared about her and did not realizes it till it was too late.

Of course it was my own fault my own stupidity you would thing I would of learned from my mistakes and you are to learn from your mistakes but I did not and could not it took more years then I care to count before I learned how to treat a girl right even to this day I am not perfect at it and my never be.

Which when my wife reads this book and I know she will the only thing I can say to her is I am sorry for not being a better person or husband and should tell you how much I care and love you! Maybe you will understand more and knowing that plus showing you how much I care is not as much as telling you.

Moving on to a regular college was quite different from going to a junior college, because of my current grade point average at the junior college I was instantly put on probation so I knew I had to work very hard to bring my grade point average up.

The culture shock was shocking non the less, I will remember my first day and my first class as if it was yesterday and will never forget the first thing I learned.

The teacher came into the class room that morning which was business management the first thing he did was go to the chalk board and he said in this class and was righting this word assume YOU WILL NOT ASSUME

IN MY CLASS why he said because if you assume here IT WILL MAKE AN ASS/OF/U/ME!!

Then he said your home work is to read the first three chapters of your book and we will have a test on Wednesday!!

I knew at that point that junior college did not prepare me for the real thing and with my learning disabilities that made it harder.

As school when on my grades still were no better then a "D" to "C" and between having classes in the morning till about 10am then leave school to go to work at Venture to about 10pm then go home and study to about 1am, go to bed and start my day all over again, so by time the weekend came I need to go out on a date or to a dance club to enjoy myself.

By time Sunday came if I was not working I studied all day did my papers get ready for tests and start my week all over again. I knew I was burning the candle at both ends and my grades suffered and at the end of my first year of college I was still on probation just keeping my grades up enough.

Starting my final year of college I had that same schedule again up at dawn and home late at night to study, I found out very fast that this schedule was not helping my grade point average and that if I could not get my grade point average up I was not going to graduate.

I started talking to one of the teachers who liked me and knew I was struggling in his class and he told me about a little class he was teaching to help you learn how to study and get better grades.

I jumped all over it and went to his class and what he was showing me was so simple it made studying easy and learning fun. As his class went on he showed me the first thing I should do after each class is to rewrite my notes and then study them, then on the second class do the same thing over and over every day re read my notes and rewrite them. This was also the same steps of reading the text book for the same class read one chapter and re read it with note taking of important points so by the time a test can you were ready.

Well it did not take me long to find out were the heck this was all my life I was able to bring up my grade point average at no time, from less than a "C" to a "C+" classes I was getting a "D" in to bring it up to a "C" and classes I was getting a "C" in to yes even a "B". I never felt so proud of myself (no one else was going to be proud of me just me) I was able to get off probation and get better grades, mind you nothing amazing but at least one grade better even a person like me with learning disabilities it made the disabilities almost bearable.

But there was one more thing I had to do the one class I enjoyed so much which was physical geography which I received a "D" in I re took that class and the teacher who also tough the how to study class which help me study better after retaking this class it.

By doing this it pushed my graduation to the following spring, but after retaking his physical geography class again my grade went from that "D" to a "B" and brought my grad point average up to a finial graduating grad point of a "C+" which I was so proud of, for me no one else was proud of me, (maybe Dad was hard to know or even remember now) but no one else was all I could do was pat myself on the back and say good job.

So as I have put emphasis on this in my book I am trying to so you that can do anything you want to as long as you put your mind to it, and growing up and graduating college way very hard for me with my disabilities but I feel it made a better person out of me more so then I could even tell anyone.

Even now as I work every day to make a better life for me and my family I can say I achieved more on my own then any one though I could and I have no one the thank but myself and a few teachers who believed in me and saw something in me and that I had more intelligent then I let on.

I will finish this chapter by pointing out how my own family was not even proud of me, again my Dad was that I know, but especially my own mother did not express joy or being happy for me or saying anything that would resemble being proud of me on my day of graduation!

On my graduation day it was a very hot day and our ceremony was in the schools garden which made it even hotter I believe it was 95F with 90% humidity with gowns on we were baking and covered in sweet.

But all I could hear was mother complaining how hot it was and how she could not stand it, but I was not going to let that stop my enjoyment of my day (that is right MY DAY) you would think someone would brought a camera and photo's of my day, no photo's of my graduation day how funny is that all I have is memories in my mind of graduation.

So let's finish my day of graduation after the ceremony we went to dinner of all places the restaurant were my mother worked as a waitress, everybody came by to talk to her and say HI how are you, but nothing was said about me and why we were there and why we were having dinner and for what reason, until the server came back to take are order and asked the question are you celebrating anything today?

Then mother said oh yes my son graduated college today and then the server said well you must be very proud of him!! But all mother said yes we are (but never said it to me! never to my face how proud she was of me) yes it hurt but it was to be expected I never got praise for any accomplishment I did so why should I think anything was going to change.

So let's just add insult to injury; I never receive a phone call from my only sister congratulating me on graduating college, of course my own sister who only took one class in junior college and never went on to finish anything she did and of course what was going to change in my life, nothing right!!

It was like my own family was jealous of what I have achieved something no one else could, lets face it I understand living in the depression families did not have money to send there kids to college they worked to survive, I get it! But this was not the times and my sister could of went to college and go a better education got a job while her husband was in the navy and made money to live on and make a better life for herself and there family.

That is why I went to college for myself to make something of myself and to show my family epically my mother and the doubting relatives I can do it were no one thought I could.

But the act of being or seeming jealous of someone achieving a goal in life is ridiculous why you can not be happy for someone. Just goes to show even a family member can be jealous or envious of their own kind.

Chapter 3

Understand in my mothers in her mind she believes that she loves her children equality and she will tell you much she loves both of her children equality, will tell you to this day.

But I know better and I am not exaggerating her love for me was always different between my sister and me which I can begin to explain how and why we were treated differently.

Growing up there were always little things I would see and notice that would tell me I was treaded differently kind of like Jeckel and Hyde. In front of family and friends mother would have this sweet and wonderful demeanor towards others everything was great or just fine in conversations anything someone said she agreed or went along and did not try to impose her will on them.

You can go up to any one of our cousins, mothers friends today and ask what they though of her and how they will tell you how wonderful she is so nice and funny such a sweet person.

But I knew better just sitting in the same room watching mother talk to other family and friends tell them sorry I do not think your are right on that this is what is right, or somebody knew about something she did not know and mother would just say really it did not know that and just go on I the conversation.

When she would be telling something she knew or believed she was right on telling me what I should do that is the right way to do things I was always wrong, I try to voice my opinion or tell her that I learned that in school make a point of what I know was right and knew what I was talking about and why I know what is correct all I would get is SHAWN!!SHAWN!!SHAWN!!

To interrupt me and not want to hear what I have to say is true, this happens all the time and almost every time I talk to her even to this day. She never wants know that I know and have more knowledge in and I know more than she does, plus what I have learned in work, life or in college meant nothing to her because in her mind I was still dumb and stupid.

Let me give an example, my mother is big into vitamins and knows everything about them (so she thinks), what to take and what not to take and if you have this problem you should take this vitamin.

At dinner while I was still in high school mother stated talking about how to lose weight and eating fat burns fat, I said that is not true mom we are taking health class in school and eating fat does not burn fat it will make you more fat you have eat lean and exercise to burn fat to lose weight.

Well let me tell you the conversation that happened next she went into her high voice and said EATING FAT BURNS FAT!!!! And then trying to get a word in edge wise was not going to happen I was wrong and what the school was teaching me was wrong and I was made to fell dumb and such a stupid thing and the teacher that was wrong for teaching us such a stupid thing.

There were many other times this would happen to me and I could tell how mother felt about me and the way I was treated even around Christmas. We would always host Christmas day at our house and have mother side of the family over. Mother would spend the whole day cleaning the house (which was already clean mother like to clean, clean and was a fanatic about that) cooking days before and all day long that day.

I was helping to bring up the chairs and the extra table for all the cousins coming over. So mother tells me to set up the card table down stairs in the basement for the kids, (we had a finished basement with a second kitchen that mom would use this and keep the up stars kitchen looking like new) you know have to preserve everything, I said to mom now that I am 21! I want to sit up in the dining room with the rest of the adults like some of the other cousins do.

Well it was like someone got killed or something like that it sounded as if the world came to an end and at that time mother went off the deep end and at the top of her voice said NO! You will sit down stairs with the other kids now and you go do as I told you do and NOW! But our other cousins are 21 and they can sit up in the dining room why not me, (I did not think mother voice could get any higher or louder.) All I got was YOU ARE SITTING DONE IN THE BASEMENT AT IS FINIAL! Wow! How do you explain how someone would feel at that moment? Like a worthless person that is not recognized as an adult to even sit with other adults and have fun conversation.

I headed down to the basement to set up the other table and chairs.

Father was down in the basement helping cook and asked what was that all about, I told him that I wanted to sit upstairs with the rest of the adults and mom went off the deep end, (dad was the master of facial expressions and jesters what he did next was priceless the look on his face only I remember how it looked and then the jester was the best) then he just said stay out of her way and help me down here.

At dinner time I was in the basement with some of the other cousins that were under 12, now do not get me wrong I love my cousins and we had a good time sitting there talking about everything but it just brought back memories of the 6th grad and being sent to the 3rd grad for reading and spelling, there are something's you really never get over.

Where was my sister at this point well the reason I am not talking about my sister is after she graduated high school and took one class of junior college she met my now brother-in-law who was in the navy, they got married and left her life behind and to start a new one, following her new husband around the country as a navy wife, you would think good right! Not really!

I will get into this more later about my sisters marriage, all I am going to say for now is that it was a good way for her so she could get away from mother, even my own sister could not stand being around mother so getting married this was what she wanted and never have to deal with mother again, you would think, but more on this later!

I want to back up again for the readers to really get the fell of why I feel the label of being a mistake is abuse and where it came to be, in the last chapter I talked about praise and how I never received any praise. Growing up no matter what was accomplishment or achieved there was never any praise and that is why today I look for it and work hard to receive and get praise.

Parents all parents give there children praise for the smallest accomplishment to the largest, children need to hear praise from there parents no matter what they do or achieve.

When a child does not receive praise they fell worthless and no matter what they do it is not good enough and there self-esteem goes out he window they begin to try less and less and before you know it they start failing at everything.

As a dad I told myself my children would never stop getting praise they were feed a steady diet of that word, the wife and I built our sons self-esteem so high they can do anything they try for our oldest son is a licensed land server and just finished his degree along with classes to achieve his licenses, and our youngest son is a executive chef.

With out our praise and support I do not think our sons would be as successful as they are today.

Around Christmas time I would always seem to have more presents under the tree then my sister which I could see why even my sister resentment of me, she would say how come he gets more than I do mom would say well we spend the same amount on both of you just his toys are less then yours.

Somehow I feel mother was trying to compensate for her own resentment or guilt in how I was treated for all those years? But I see that mother cared more for my sister because I could see that my sister could do nothing wrong and it would always hear your sister this and my sister that, or poor, poor sister I would here all the time.

In explaining my story of how I was treated as a child growing up which dose not give you the hole history of why the resentment from my own mother of who I am and why

I feel this strongly about this label of being called a mistake and the abuse I received.

Even to this day and I am over 60 I still am not treated as an adult with any respect and of the knowledge I have and learned, plus what I know more then some people who claim to know every thing, even then my own mother which never gives me an ounce of respect, or credit. She does not listen to me when I give my opinion or answer to her question or when I know the answer to what she is asking about, mother will not listen to me and never have and never will.

But let's get in to where this all started in my life so you can understand what I am talking about.

As a child grows up you start developing who you are with your own personality mannerisms and such, which I feel is were the abuse started and the resentment began. See being a baby or a toddler you are controlled told what to do and when to do it and how to do it but once my mother started to loose that control is were the abuse and resentment really started.

I started to understand the "I was a mistake" when I was about 8 years old or so, as Italians there are parties for every occasion, all the men depends on the time of year on a nice warm weather they would site outside in lawn chair talking about work and the war smoking cigarettes or cigars and of course drinking, typical stereotype Italians and waiting for the food to be ready.

Then the women would sit in the kitchen talking smoking and drinking wine and complaining about their husbands, which sounds about normal in every day life. Then the kids they were put in a room to either play games or watch TV and stay out of the way of the adults. My sister and I would sit play board games with our consents or walk around outside.

But there was a very special party one time I walk into the kitchen to get something to drink and was listen to the women talk about there kids, mother took this moment to start talking about us and how proud she was with my sister and how smart she was in school and her good grades she was getting.

Then mother got to me "well she said we only want one child and was not planning on having a second child but whoops I was pregnant with Shawn we did not plan on him he was a MISTAKE"!! And with that my mother looked right at me with this anger in her eyes that I cannot even begin explain was she trying to be funny, but I could see and feel the resentment in her face and tone of here voice on how she felt.

Maybe you think I am over exaggerating but if you could see what I saw and how it was said you would understand how I felt leaving the kitchen. This was not the only time my mother said this about me there was another time later at the family pick nick were the men were playing house shoes and the women were sitting around just talking and I came by again, and the same story started up with the same results.

Shawn was a MISTAKE we did not plan on him; I could felt my own mother resented me because of my learning disabilities and how embarrassed she was that her only son was failing in school. I only remember maybe one other time she used this label, but how do you say that about you own child in front of family and friends.

So as I talked about my life going thru school and how I was left on my own with no support or love how you would think a child growing up with no confidence or self worth would even succeed in life get a job and support a family.

As a young person I became very determined and was not going to let anything stop me even in high school, the more I was made fun of and my own mother making me fell as a mistake this only fuelled my determination on working very hard to not fail and I was going to show my parents especially mother that I would never failure and no matter what I had to do failure was not a option. I would not even give my mother the satisfaction of knowing that I failed at something and work hard every day to accomplish what I started and to finish it so I would not here those words I told you so!

The more I was told that I could not do something the more I worked at achieving what I was told I could not do.

Even to this day never tell me I cannot do something this will get me very angry and will do anything to prove to you I can do it. For example I was laid off from job during a very down time in the economy in 2009 and my wife said you will never get a job in this economy what are your going to do for an income? How are you going to support us, never tell me I will not get a job or fail at something?

I worked as if I was possessed to get a new job, the wife had a part time job working for a hospital which helped keep us going and along with a part time bartender job which help and what unemployment was not giving me.

I would spend every waking moment on the computer looking for work, never stop never gave up, I must of sent out over 300 resumes over that period of time that took about 5 months in a bad economy to get a new job! Not bad right!! You think someone would be proud of me and say things like I am very happy for you, or I am proud of you or even I knew you could do it! But nothing like that ever was said. All I got from mother was "Oh good are you making more money and how far are you driving for this new job".

But if this was my sister and her husband lost his job you know mother she would be on the old band wagon say my poor, poor daughter they have no money for food or to pay their bills and out would come the check book and she would sent them a check so they would get by for a week or so.

By having my own drive and building my own self confidence going thru my early life this would not be easy for someone who never received self confidence or any support.

But there would be sometimes that I would get confidence and self worth from my friends, teachers and other people I knew, in the early years you do not have this self worth and self a steam but only what you feel and get from your parents, this was hard for me because I never got a lot of this from my parents especially from my mother who never made me feel good about myself or even wanted, most of the time I was made to feel worthless.

On the other hand my father was not around much he worked grave yard shift most of my life and not around to help much and only on weekends.

Are special times together of course I was doing yard work mowing the grass working in the garden trimming the bushes and there was a few times we play golf together not much but I wish we did.

Yes sounds like all I was good for is nothing but labor, but this did one thing for me it showed me how to take care of my own home and keep it nice and well groomed my grass is like a carpet with no weeds and my neighbors follow what I do for my yard and try to keep up with me, because my yard is a show case and I will thank my dad for showing me how to take care of my home and yard.

I really can not tell you went my father stop working grave yard shift but I believe it was around when I started in junior high school or high school, kind of nice having someone home at night.

There were so many years coming home from school and dad and I would warm up dinner that mother had prepared earlier in the day.

I never really got away from my past until junior college where I really found myself stating new at high school was still the same group of class mates knowing my past and what they could do to exploit my problems and spread it around my new high school.

But in Junior college was a place I found what I wanted to do with myself and carrier. I took business courses and the basic college courses that would move me into a regular college and get my degree in business management. Developing my own personality and growing more and more confident in myself I really developed who I was and what I wanted to be, with out any help from my mother or anyone.

Needing to earn my own money to pay my way thru college I started to look of work, one of the first places I went to was a tire store and though the hours there could support me working and going to school. Well mother would not here of it, all I got was how you going to earn any money selling tires!! Do you know how long I have had mine tires! You cannot make any money doing that. Yes great self confident's booster you know mother, then she proceeded to tell me that the grocery store one the corner was looking for stock boys.

I know the owner she said I will get you that job (great sell tires was below a stock boy at a grocery store), this was a way she could control me again telling were to work and how to earn money. (Remember I talked about this job earlier in this book), as a person trying to be independent I did not like mother going around me and talk to the owner to get me this position, though let's try it so I took it anyway got the job and showed the owner and my mother that I was not slouch and work very hard and did very well.

After a year I had enough of that kind of work and moved over to our local bank and got a job as of all things another stock boy, another word for gofer running earns and doing jobs no one else wanted to do which I liked doing basely because I was my own boss unless someone wanted something done or for me to go and get what was ever needed.

It was a good place to work part of my duties were to shredding documents, doing the mail even running down town Chicago to deposit large checks at the main bank.

I think that was a start of my own self confidences, that a bank they trusted me to do my job; of course mother never said anything positive just negative comments, but I could tell father was proud of me getting a better job making more money and good hours to work.

This job was also good because of the hours I could go to college and work at the same time as well as having my own control of paying my own college bills and money if I wanted to go out, mother would lose more control over me and I know she hated that. Which is what I wanted more than anything, but living under the same roof she was still thinking she had control.

The more control over me she lost the more it felt as she resented me so by the time I was ready to get married and move out on my own mother still tried imposed her will on me and my wife soon to be trying to control everything and even the wedding plans.

Which just about ruined everything and made my fiancée very sick and nearly broke us up, mother had to have things her way. My fiancée wanted no children at the reception and I agreed because we were paying for everything.

But mother had to have her grand kids, nieces and nephews at the reception she said I will pay for them but that was not the point we told everyone on both sides children not invited, so how would that look to others not bring their kids to the reception.

As you would of guess mother won out on this and got her way, I can still keep going mother also wanted a sweet table, we did not want one and another fight broke out as you could of guessed, you heard of the term bridezilla well

I give my now wife credit for putting up the mother of all motherzillas!!!

Again this is all about control with my mother trying to control everything in my life no one else but mine control everything in my life and it was killed her not to be in control of anything.

Let's be honest I could not wait for my wedding day just so this hell would be over with and I would be out on my own and away from mother.

Of course you never really get away from them you have to be around them for every holiday and every birthday and family gathering. But at least I go home to my own house and not back to their home and have to keep dealing with it.

But anytime I wanted dad to come by and help me with something around my new house mother had to tag along.

There was one time dad came over to help me to put up the TV antenna on the house, we also had my mother and father in law over along with mother, what a fiasco that was three women in the kitchen making dinner for us when we were done on the roof.

I did not know where my father in law was I think he though better then be in the house he must have been outside walking around even holding the ladder just to make it look as if he was doing something!

Dad and I could hear all the yelling and loud talking on the roof we just looked at each other and we both knew what each other was thinking! But we did not have to say a thing!

Chapter 4

So let's talk about my one and only sister I am not sure where our relationship when south but as we were growing up we had a normal brother and sister type of thing going on fighting over toys, or games who cheated who did not.

But being the oldest by two years she was in charge of me coming home from first grade we would get out of school together and walk home. Because mother worked not sure if she really need to but mother did not want to sit home and be a stay at home mom.

My sister would have the key and sis would open the door and then we would not leave the house till mother got home yes there were some days mother would pick us up but most of the time we walk home.

Of course when winter set in there were other arraignments had to be made mother was there to take us home and then she would got to work, very funny arrangement.

Now remember I am going on memory I could be a little off on all of this but I know my sister was in charge of me when mother was not around as we were very young and what I do know of what I am saying is true.

As we moved out of our old place we move to another western suburb were dad built a custom home, I was 8 by that time and by then I was given my own key and rode my bike to school all year round. Yes that is right I rode my bike do not remember how far it was but in the winter it was tuff riding a bike in the snow and cold, (now I know where I get my dislike for winter) I was riding my bike in all kinds of weather.

I would were out a set of bike tiers before I would out grow my bike in warmer weather I would go back and forth to school for lunch my lunch would be set in the refrigerator I would come home and let the dog out eat lunch and go back to school.

You ask where is my sister in all of this, funny you should ask she did not ride her bike back and forth to school not sure if she even did ride her bike to school I thinks she started using the buses right at the start the school year?

But of course it was up to me to ride my bike back and forth to school coming home taken care of our dog and my sister the prima donna heaven forbid would have to ride her bike, and she resented me! I should be the one with resentment but no I never resented my sister for nothing.

I just want a sister to talk to and have a good friend and be able to tell her anything and someone just to hang with and have a good time but that never happened! I grew up with out a sister and a mother too very hard for a person non the less a child to deal with this.

So let's get back to a dog that is right mom had to have a dog a little Schnauzer called snoopy as you remember in the begging of this book I have very bad allergies to all types of animals with fir and dander but Schnauzers had hair and which does not bother my allergies at all.

So of course all the responsibility fell on me I made sure the dog would go out, make sure it was fed, bathed and taken care of, mother's dog but I did all the work she never paid attention to the dog unless it was in the way and she wanted to clean or it made a mess.

But as you would guess since I was taken care of the dog I fell in love with her (sorry if I did not mention snoopy was a girl) and she became attached to me followed me everywhere I went. I went to bed she would follow I did my home work she laid at my feet, cutting the grass she had to be outside watching me, snoopy was my best friend and I loved her so much.

But back to my sister you ask were was my sister all the time I did not know she would go to school and did not care about letting the dog out because she came home after school and would most of the time stay in her room and do home work and then would come out for dinner. She would not sit and watch much TV with dad and me; sis would do typical girl things like sit on the phone and talk to her friends.

My sister did not have to worry about watching me now because I was on my own with my own key coming and going by myself.

So buy 6th grade and school buses came into play I would leave in the morning and come home at 3:30pm and dad was gone at work and mother did not leave for work till about noon so our dog could be left till I came home to let her out and then I warm up the food and ate dinner then I did my home work, my sister was home taking care of herself and if I needed help yep you guessed it I was on my own, there was some help but mostly none.

This went on thru high school I would come home very day and take care of the dog and warm up dinner and so when I started high school my sister was a senior and cannot remember what and when she ever came home she would not take the bus her friends would driver her home and she would be in her room or out with her friends.

Buy the time I was a sophomore and my sister had graduated high school and took one class at the local junior college she was nineteen and then met her now husband and my brother in law who was in the navy.

It was not long after they met and they got married and my sister was on her way out of the house to follow him all over the US to be where ever he was stationed. But you know when she left to get married it was as I said her perfect way out of the house away from mother because she told me that she could not stand being around her and was glade to be away from her, this was probably the last time she would say anything to me as a sister would talk to her brother.

What she said still rings in my ear today she said "I cannot wait to get married and get the hell away from mother" no sooner married they left the next day on their honey moon and I would say my sister would never come back again, but when she did came back around when it was convent like needing money a place to say when she was passing thru and someone to watch the grand kids.

The only time my sister would call home was to cry to mother how broke she was and lonely because her husband was out to sea for months at a time and of course mother would buy into it and would send her money and say "oh your poor, poor sister does not have any money and can not get work".

As you would have guessed every week on the phone to mother crying the blues, but when she did call you would think my sister would say "hey put my brother on I want to talk to him" heck no! I would have to ask can I talk to sis and of course the phone conversation would last about 30 seconds and she would say good bye to mom and that would be it she got her weekly check from money.

So where did this resentment come from? That is a good question I have no idea. I feel it started to happen when got married and bought my own home and could stand on my own two feet.

When I got married my sister came in and stood up in the wedding which was a surprise to me but after that a brother sister relationship was never there.

Since she lived out of state there was very little to no contact with her my wife tried to some kind of contact on birthdays, my wife would send birthday cards and Christmas cards but half the time my sister would never send a card or it come and be very late. I would ask mom what is with my sister not sending us a birthday or Christmas cards all I my mother would do is make an excuses for her "oh your sister can not afford to send you and your wife cards" really I though her own brother cannot send a 25cent card, yah right it was mother way of my poor poor sister cannot afford anything and more crying the blues.

You know I really think this is where the resentment came from it was because my wife and I have build a good foundation of a life we both worked made enough money to put down on a home and have are feet planted and able to do things on are own "which I said earlier".

Not like my sister moving from place to place because my brother in law was in the navy, Oh but what I minuet I did not explain one thing about my brother in law being in the navy he was not drafted when the time came he joined the navy for four years this was a good way to get college credit when he got out.

My sister could not stand him being going for months on end and by that time they had two children money was always short and being a navy man the pay was not good so of course my sister cried to mother and told her that they wanted to get a lawyer to get her husband out of the Navy on a hardship case this would be a dishonorable discharge which mother went to father to borrow $3,000 to pay the attorney have done.

I know this really made dad mad he did not say anything but I could see it in his face, because my father being a Navy man himself fighting in WWII and not running from his reasonability and finishing his tour of duty like a real man would and this would really eating dad up inside.

So back to my sister, when I graduated college I never got a phone call a card or anything to say congratulations on finishing college. I think all I got was mom was on the phone with sis and she said your sister said nice going on graduating or something like that??

The more and more I think I believe the resentment turns into jealousy because of what I was doing with my life and my sister was always struggling in her marriage and always running to mother for money and help, not to say it was easy for me but my wife and I did it ourselves also I was working two jobs for over 28 years of our married life my wife may of stayed home to raise our son's but she did baby sitting at home to bring in extra money too, so we did a lot on our own without much help from mother or from the in laws.

My income was nothing to talk about but with both of us working and with extra money we made it helped us get thru the tuff times.

But my mother would never say to me "oh you should quite working your second job OH NO! It was always are you working this weekend oh good I hope you make money" I was giving up my nights and weekends where I wanted to be around my own sons. I was ok for me to work 10 to 12 hours on a Saturday night bartending, but you would think mother would tell my lazy sister get off your butt and get a job.

My sister never worked a full time job at all in her married life just one time she worked a real job for an insurance company I believe it was only part time too not sure so do not hold me to it because my sister never talked to me about anything, and mother kept everything hiding from me about what my sister did just the parts were she was so broke all the time, this job my sister took was just to save money so she could get a pool for their house and then quiet the job once she got the pool.

You think mother would tell her not to waste her money on a pool and keep working to bring in money NO! Everything my sister did was so right! If there was something we need to buy for the house or go on vacation mother would stick her nose in and tell us why are you needing to buy that and you should not go on vacation and spend all that money.

When Christmas time came around I would get a list of things to buy my nephews but when we gave them a list of things to buy my sons all we got were some used toys that the nephews out grew and did not want anymore of course all I would hear from mother saying your sister cannot afford to buy your kids anything but it was ok for us too! Nice really a good way to treat your own children as equals! It was always a very one sided mother's love for her daughter and not her son, OH no she would swear up and down how much she love her children the same and treated us the same.

As you read my book do you think she treated her children the same I let you be the judge of that and what I am telling you. I am not exaggerating about anything this is the truth as I remember it which burned into my memory and I did say I could be a little off on some things.

I have seen proof of my own mother send my sister a check almost every week or every month, mother would call every week to see how she was doing and how's the grand kids and then my sister would go into singing the blues how she has no money for food and money for clothes for them and mom would say how much do you need to get by then mom would get her check book out and write a check for $300 to $400 dollars.

Now you may think I am exaggerating again but I saw mother's check book and I would flip thru the pages of the ledger and there would be a checks written to my sister almost every week or every month of the amount I just told you.

So you think that was enough but somehow no it was not, when mother would send my wife and me a check for Christmas is would be for $200, and going thru the ledger on her check book there were check's for $500 and as much as $750!!! So where was the equality?

You may ask yourself how did get my hands on my mother's check book ledgers well mother made the mistake asking me and the wife to help clean out all her bank statements and check book ledgers that she was saving for years. So you know I started looking thru them and what I saw was priceless and socking at the same time.

Then you ask yourself why would your sister have a resentment for me, well as I said with the money the wife and I made we did not waste it we made extra payments to our home mortgage and paid off a 15 year mortgage in less than 10 years.

When you have that monkey off your back your paychecks is all yours to do what you want with and not worry about a mortgage is a great feeling, so you ask what did I do with my paychecks well some people may say invest it in the stock market or something like that, but that was not for me.

So I talked it over with the wife and we decided to purchase investment property and rent it out, and YES I though it out and knew renters do not care about your property and knew there would be problems but was willing to deal with it. But we did not purchase an investment property in Illinois we went to Las Vegas Nevada and stated shopping around, not on our own but found the perfect real state agent and spend one day until we found the perfect home it was in a gated community of townhomes four townhomes to a building two story with three bed rooms just 2 miles off the strip and south of the main Las Vegas strip by 20minuts it was just perfect.

I hired and fired property Management Company's over the 10 years we own it and we still own the town home to this day and after 10 years we had enough of renters and then turned it into a vacation home just for us to use.

Plus the wife and I did not stop there we also purchased a patio home in Goodyear Arizona and rented it out as well for almost as many years as we did with the home in Las Vegas but when we turn our home in Vegas to a vacation home after 10 years we decided to sell the home in Goodyear Arizona.

But wait it gets better as we were doing this purchasing of these investment properties and renting them out and then turning the property in to a vacation home you would think my mother would be proud of me for doing something like this, you would think but NO all my mother would say was "why are you doing this you need to sell those homes and get rid of them you do not need to have rental homes or a vacation home you are wasting your money".

Tell me does this sound like mother proud of her son and daughter in law NO it does not, all I hear is jealousy and resentment of me and my wife that we could be that smart to do something like at, and to this day anytime something comes up about money my mother will start telling me to get rid of those homes and why do you have them! What love and such support for her son! You may wonder were my father at this point well he had died in 1994.

So this is where I feel my sister deep resentment and jealousy of her only brother, this developed and started her though process of finding the ways of stabbing me in the back and steel every bit of my father's inheritance from me and thinking she was entitled to it because we were doing well and independent and they were not.

Because of what my wife and I could do with little money and a little hard work and of course that is the word "a little work" something my sister did not know anything about, stayed home to raise the nephews and when they were 18 kick them out of the house did not pay or help pay for their college or even help them to buy a car nothing you're on your own now.

We help our sons with their college and help with their first cars but I said with a car come great reasonability, when my son's wanted a car they had to have a job to pay for all the expenses of that car no free ride and both of my son's have a great knowledge of the value of a dollar I am very proud of them and how they grew up to be responsible adults.

Just to clear the inheritance thing up a bit my father died in September of 1994 and of course left everything to mother (big mistake dad big mistake) opened up the check book for my sister, for 20 years after dad passed my sister was still looking for money from mother and I know she was sending it, once a moocher always a moocher, she could not stand on her own two feet even if she had to and the same with the bother in law too.

Back to this inheritance thing before father passed way he put his custom built home up for sale and he was asking a I felt a fare amount for it a little high but he felt it was worth it a full brick home with hot water heating, but there were draw backs to the home a master bedroom with no bath room the hall bath, no formal dining room and the big thing was no central air.

It made it hard to sell but father dies before it was sold leaving mother in charge of sell it, but of course mother would not confide in me about pricing or selling it she listened to the real estate agent and gave it away.

She bought a two bedroom town home and lived there but who do you think took care of things for mother yes that is right me! For 20 years after father passed I would go over to her house to change light bulbs fix leaking faucets and running toilets.

Plus remember my sister did not live in Chicago she lived in the south moving from home to home changing address like changing my socks every couple of year's new home new address.

I had mother over for every holiday Christmas, Thanksgiving, Easter and every birthday, mother's day, and included her when I had my father in law over for this birthday and fathers day.

You ask where is my sister living out of town nowhere to be found mother at my house and my sister never called my house to wish us a happy holiday and just remember sis hardly ever call mother for anything mother called her 90% of the time, on mother's day mother would call sis to wish her a happy mother's day and then would say happy mother's day to her. Plus sis would not send mother a card for most things maybe just maybe Christmas and of course noting in it and mother would say "oh poor daughter she cannot afford to send a card or put any money in it but she does not have to because she cannot afford it".

As always making excuses for her which became a regular thing, and when my sister was invited to anything like weddings, graduations or birthday parties mother would get a card and put money in it and put my sisters and brother in laws name on the card and say it was from them.

So if I sound bitter, I am just look at how my mother treated my sister over me I have stood on my own for two feet all of my life never asking anyone for a hand out worked two jobs for 28 years of marriage and the wife working multiple part time jobs along with a full time one just so we can make ends meet. Along comes my sister and is handed everything and even more as I will get in to soon.

Here is another example of mother one sidedness for my sister over me, I was living is a southern suburb of Chicago place called Bolingbrook I was driving to work all the way to Addison this was 30 miles one way and was expensive on gas and the my car was getting old and I was going to trade the car in on a small compact car to save on gas and repairs but mother said I will buy your care and you will have more money to put down on you new car.

Well how about that mother comes to help? Not really! It was all a scam to buy my car from me and give "that is right" gives my car or now my mother's car to my sister who needs a car for free.

How about that who gives you a fee car not me yes the little extra I got for my car help with the paying of the new car we needed but still I took money out of my account to purchase this car! And my sister never had to take a dime out of her pocket for that car.

Ask yourself how would you feel if one of your parent was treating one of your siblings better then you and you were treated as a un wanted child, sure I would totally understand if I was adopted and would not feel so bad about being treated this way or any worst then now.

As I back up here a little bit I said my father past 20 years ago leaving mother everything, as time was going on mother by this time has reached her limit of living alone she was 93 losing her hearing and mobility and her ability to drive a car.

Mother was knocking off her mirrors to her car as she was pulling out of the garage and not pulling up in the garage enough and the garage door as it comes down it would hit the car. Plus hitting other cars and blaming it on someone else hitting her car, mother must have had the mechanic and body shop on speed dial because they were constantly fixing her car.

At this time my sister and I were talking once a week regularly which was a shock to me she was so sincere about getting mother to live with one of us, and we talked about mom and how she could not be alone anymore which I thought my sister was going to start acting like a sister but Whoops silly me this was all a plan to get mother to move in with her.

I called every time something happened to mother fall and break her wrist in the house because she had her shoes on. But who took care of her my wife and I did, we took her to the doctors when shopping for her went over and help clean the house and do laundry, whatever that was needed do you think she appreciated it no she made it sound as if we did not want to help her.

So as time when on I keep telling mom you cannot live alone anymore told her she could move in with me or sis, but she would not have anything to do with it I can take care of myself she said. Yah sure mom look at you we are coming over a couple of times a week just to help you.

Then mother needed her knee replaced because it was so bad mother could not walk any more so she had it replaced and after surgery she went into a nursing home for rehab and to get back on her feet. Well guess who would run over there two or three times a week? Yes you are right I did and so did the wife pick up some of her dirty laundry and wash them bring them back and then visit for a while.

But ask your self were was my sister in all of this you are right no were to be found would not call mom but mother would call her so I call her and asked if she was coming out to say with mom for a few weeks when she was released and she said she would, I said great give us a break.

But mother had to be cleared by the nursing home to go home and be able to move around the house and take care of herself so there was weeks of therapy and when it came time to get evaluated mother and I sat down with the staff of the nursing home and talk about mother. They quested me how and who will be with her as she is at home I said my sister will be coming in for two weeks to stay with her while she continues her therapy and walks with or without a walker.

Well here comes the best part and this will prove to you the reads and for the reason why that I am writing this book and how my life has been and the ongoing abuse I have had to deal with growing up with this person who I call mother, and why mother never wants to hear what I have to say and does not want to believe anything I say it true.

As we discussed how my mother was progressing in her therapy one of the social worker told me and my mother at this stage in your life and since you had this knee replacement and your ability to get around without a walker the social worker told us that my mother should no longer live alone.

But my mother said "oh is do not want to do that I do not want to be responsible to ruin my children's marriage" but the social worker insist that mother should live with one of use. So after we left the nursing home and I got mom home I started to discuss what the social worker said.

As you would of guessed mother denied everything the social worker said and mother started yelling at me saying "she never said that and said nothing about living with anyone!!!" I said WHAT!! Yes they did I was right there are you calling me a liar she said that to both of us you even told her you would not want to live with one of your children. Mother again denies anything the social worker said and again said "she never said that".

Well with at this time 58 years of pent up anger and abuse with years of lies and insults I just could not stand it anymore and went off the deep end and started yelling at the top of my voice "YOU ARE CALLING ME A LIER YOU

AND I WERE THERE TOGETER HOW DARE YOU CALL ME A LIER" among other adjectives I was using.

This was not the only time I lost it with mother a few weeks later after my sister left to go back home mother needed to go to her doctor for a follow up. So as the doctor was finishing her exam he started telling her that you know if you have that option to live with one of your children it is a good idea and an option you should take and live with one of them.

Again mother said "oh no I cannot move in with any of my children I don't want to ruin their marriage and be a bother" plus this was right in front of the nurse. So as we were checking out and getting her next visit set up with the same nurse I said see mom your doctor even thinks you should not be living along anymore and again my mother denied ever hearing anything the doctor said and again said he never said that!!

As you would expect I again lost it how dare you call me a lire right in front of the nurse who was in the room. All my mother would say to the nurse was my son is never like this he is always so kind and nice and never yells I do not know what his problem is.

Well that just infuriated me more how dare you lie like that you do not want to hear the truth of what the doctor said, mom said again he never said that your making that up. I looked at the nurse and said do you believe this you were there you hear it. The nurse said my father was like that he did not want to give up his independence. I said she would not be giving up anything just her ability to drive a car, yes I know the nurse said they think they can still do everything.

I said to the nurse my mother does not drive now for months even before she got her knee replaced I drove everywhere she had to go to one of her doctors or go shopping I would take her car and drive her to do all the shopping and doctor visits how is that independent!! The nurse said that is how they are as long as they still have a car they think they are still independent.

As conversation when on with my sister by phone on a weekly basses I thought my sister was acting like a concerned sister about mom wanting to know what is going on how she is doing at home by herself. I would just tell her that my wife I are running over to her house two to three times a week doing thinks for her, washing clothes, cleaning the house shopping bring over food so she does not have to cook for herself.

Well my sister said "mother is due to get her driver's license she will fail it and then she will not be able to drive and then will have to move in with one of us" yah right that did not happen somehow one the cousins helped her to get to the DMV and take her test and of all things pass the driver's license test.

You tell me how does the DMV allow a at that time 90 plus years old lady that is hard of hearing that cannot hold a steering wheel at 10 and 2 plus able to turn her head to see over her shoulder and do the over the hand over hand turning of the car??? How does that happen? I believe the last straw was when mom pulled out of the garage to get her hair and nails done which she liked to go every week she pulled out of the garage and proceeded to pull the door trim off the garage door and almost pull her mirror off her car.

But in just a few weeks she had a handy man come by and fix the door trim and her body ship fix her car mirror.

Then my sister said take mom's car keys away before she hurts someone that is the last time I want to hear mom do something like that.

So like a good stooge I did!! I took both sets of keys away and I cough hell for it. Yelling and screaming at me saying how you can do this to me you are a bad son for doing this and then telling all the relatives what kind of bad son I was.

I said sorry mom if you need to go somewhere my wife or I will do it for you besides taking the key's way was your daughter's idea! But of course mother made it sound that I did this alone and my sister had nothing to do with it telling everyone she could how bad I was, go figure I was the one for 20 years taking care of her but I was the bad one because I did not want her to kill someone with her car, sure my sister never gave a hoot about mother just send me a check when I need it but I was the bad one.

But as you would expect mother had a third set of key's how wonderful this person on the road that is a danger to others. Still made at me for taking away her keys mother would still have our cousins take her to the doctors and shopping and not even ask me or my wife to help.

Making me looks like the bad guy in front of everyone but yet I was hearing how someone else scraped her car in the parking lot at church and she had to get it fixed. Yah right mother I would say just you all the time someone hitting your car in the parking lot sure I believe that.

This went on for another year and my sister and I just talked on the phone as she though mother would fail her next driver's test again. But with the help of my cousins you just could not leave well enough alone and just keep helping her get her license, which should have not been there concern mother was a danger to other drivers on the road, plus no one had any control over her to just tell her no! We will not help you this is not our place to do this. I feel they must have thought if it makes her happy she should keep her license! But wait!! This is my mother and I should have the say so if mother should have a drivers license or not, but of course with mother's way of telling all the family and friends that I am stupid and not capable of making any intelligence's decisions the cousins thought they should just take over my authority of being the head of the family.

Mother had a very good friends and they did everything together they went bowling; out to lunch, visited other friends. Everything you would want and elderly person to have as they got older other people to be with and not lonely which I thought this was great. It keep mother busy and out of my hair.

But as I talked about the older mother got the less she was going out she would stay in the house for weeks on end and was only talking to her good friend because as mother's friend was getting older she was losing her eye site.

Until one day mother's friend passed away and I believe this was the point in mother's life when her best friend was gone she had nothing or any reason to say in her home in Illinois and called my sister and told her to come and get me I and that she was going to move in with her in Georgia.

I believe this was my sister's master plan for the ATM machine to move to Georgia with her, yes I said mother is now her ATM and why do I say this first my sister was never good with money and she is in over her head with her embroidering business. As a business man I know what it takes to run you own business and especially when you buy as franchise and then buy a second one.

As a franchise owner you buy the name so what my mother does not know I am not stupid and I did more investigating to the point of finding out how much my sister paid for her franchise business.

I was told by the company if you want to be a franchise owner of Embroidering franchise it cost $170,000 and you can finance it with $50,000 of you own money down and pay the rest on time and if the business is good no problem to pay it back. After a few years my sister and brother in law purchased a second franchise which cost them another $170,000 with the down payment of $50,000.

Ok you ask me how I know this is what my sister is doing and what I know is right, well it is right because she never in her life had enough money to pay it in full or purchase anything without going into debit.

My wife and I could and we did things the right way even when we purchased our rental property we were smart we made sure we could make the mortgage payments if they were not rented, how you ask? It was because our current home was paid in full, yes we paid off our current mortgage and the bank gave us a loan to purchase them and when the homes were rented the rent paid the mortgage with money left over for anything else that may need to be paid for.

Now if found out that one of my sisters embroidering business failed and she had to close it up and remove everything inventory and machines you could not sell the inventory or machines back to the franchise. Why you ask not sure depends on how the contact is written with the company and my sister said she had to rent a place to store all this stuff.

So now she is into the franchise company for at least $120,000 plus the one she owns now and I estimate at one time she was in debit some were around $240,000 and only one business running to pay back this amount.

My mother lives with my sister and pays her $600 dollars a month to live there, (funny my mother in law lives with my for free!)

Plus my mother would complain she does not have any money to give out Christmas, birthday or anniversary gifts! Really my mother social security check is over $1,800 a month so were that money going to? I can only guess.

As you can see this hole plan was my sisters way of getting all of my fathers inheritance away from mother and take it way from me.

So let me keep going, about 10 years ago my brother in law lost his sales position with a good company called Fry Master not sure on everything in this position as you know I was always keep in the dark about anything my sister and brother in laws life, I will never know the truth about anything in my sisters life mother made sure of this because she told me whatever she felt and I believe to this day it was all lies and just partial truth.

Now in this position he traveled all the time going to trade shows sell their products. Which I know traveling is tuff on families especially when you are gone for weeks at a time.

I was told by mother that my brother in law went into his bosses' office and asked to travel less and she said he was promptly fired!

Really I believe that on when pig can fly! who in any job ask to do less travel and get's fired for it?? I have been in the business and have seen everything of over 20 years even as a purchasing manager that if you go into your boss and requests something he or she will say ok or tell you this is your job you do as I need you to do or find another job and you do what you need to do I know I have been there before.

So tell me why did he get let go for just asking something simple as wanting to travel less? I feel he was not doing his job well enough and was removed from his position weather my brother in law was doing his job efficient or not I do not know the truth and may never know because as I said before I have been lied to and lead to believe something with wrong information.

What ever happened only they know and I will never know the true story, I have been lied to and not knowing the truth about what goes on in their lives. But mother needs to know everything about my life and what goes on and what I get or do not get just so my sister gets more help then I have in my life, but I have never asked for help or even implied I need any help.

Even when I was out of work twice over the last five years mother never asked if I needed anything or do I need any help. You can see that the one sidedness and always my poor, poor sister, never poor. Poor Shawn who has worked two jobs for over 28 years of my married life to help make ends meet and my wife working most of her married life to help bring in a income to help out.

Let me make this clear I am not jealous of my sister and yes I sound like I am which I am not you need help sure but there comes a time you need to stand on your own two feet and there is a time you say your on your own both of you need to get a real job and work! But the ATM machine will take care of you.

No just my poor sister who now for the last 10 years of her marriage has to work owning her own business that does embroidering along with my brother in law. That never lost a job before and what!! Cannot go out and get a new one, I have had to and have done several times over my 20 plus years in purchasing loose a job get a new one it is not hard to do if you are will to put in an effort for it and work hard for it. Which I have always had to work hard and work extra to make a living! Just some people think they are entitled to a free ride in life and a hand out and know someone will be helping you all the time.

So my sister has this business which is a franchised business and which I know all about franchised businesses and what is initialed in owning one. But my mother who has been feed a bunch of lies and she acts as if she is an authority on owning a business even a franchised business.

But mother likes to tell me all about my sisters business "you know your sister has to travel to a trade shows every year in Las Vegas and her company pays for it" Like what!! I said no mother our sister owns a franchise business and pays for it out of her pocket to go to trade shows no matter where they are and they write it off at the end of year as part of doing business.

Well we all know what is coming next "NO, NO, NO her company pays for it" and I said that is right her company pays for it NOT the franchise!! Her company and she pay's for business trips. Yes mother you do not get it remember I went to college and have been in business and working in business for over 40 years of my life and I know these things.

Should I of expected anything different for the past 60years of my life I do not know anything I am stupid! I when to college!! No one else did and I know absolutely nothing about business I even studied business and my major is business.

Yes this is my sister and brother in laws business and the franchise they own from the main company they will get special deals on travel and hotels of course I know that but it is not paid for by the company who they by the franchise from.

Then I get all the stories on how my sister has to work 7 days a week and put in all those hours of works along with my brother in law. Really I said are they open 7 days a week?? Yes my mother said they work so many hours and days. As you know I never believe anything I am told by my mother, she thinks I am too dumb to investigate so go in to my sisters embroidering web page! And what do I see open 5 days a week and hours of operation something like 9 to 5pm daily.

So who is fooling who, as far as I can tell and for the number of years and of which has been many. I do not know how many lies in my life that I have been told of these false stories and lies to hide things from me and not to tell me the truth of anything at all. Let tell Shawn lies and stories he is to dumb and stupid he will never figure out the truth or even look into it!

Well I am not as dumb as they think I am, there are things I know I will never let on I know, the truth comes out from family and friends, and believe that my own mother would lie to her own son and to think I do not have enough intelligent to know anything in life or about life it's self.

Mother has even said to me as we argued over this she said to me "it is a franchise dummy"!! Like I do not know that is said that's what I have been tell you all this time and remember I went to college and I know all about franchises!

Since father has passed the lies and stories have increased many times over, I feel mother never wants me to know anything about my sister and what is going on in there her life and what mother has given her and done for her over the years and what mother has said she has done for me which is not much.

With that being said the out pouring of more lies keep coming as mother lived in Georgia, I keep hearing how my sister was going to retire and stay home to take care of mom, remember I still have not talked to my sister since mother moved to Georgia.

So let me elaborate on this subject now as mother live in Illinois I had a copy of mother's last will and testament saying everything would be split equal between my sister and me of ever thing father left behind. But as soon as mother moved to Georgia everything changed all of a sudden there was a new will changing everything such as all my mother positions and property belongs to my sister, really!! Property my mother has no property?? But wait yes she does! As I find out my sister was sell her home to buy a three thousand plus square foot home so I asked mother why there should be plenty of room for just 3 of you, so you know what I got as an answer? Yes you gusset it more lies, as she said "your sister needs a bigger home because they do not have a bathroom with a shower because I cannot lift my leg to get into the bathtub also the bathroom is not big enough for me and if they want to make the hall bathroom into something I can use it will cost them over $16,000 dollars to build".

Ok really mother must think I am really stupid if you think it would cost that much to redo the bathroom I will come down and do it for half that cost. I would love to know how my bother in law could feed my mother that kind garbage and think I would even believe that.

Well no matter how much I want to explain or even say that price is way out of line, I keep getting shot down and my intelligent was getting insulted and attacked.

As someone knowing a lot about re molding and purchasing, I know that even if you gut the bathroom right down to the studs and bare floor you could not even get close to $6,000 dollars.

The wife wanted our master bathroom re molded and all we did was remove the shower and the entire tile on the wall was replaced the shower faucet and all plumbing plus painting including labor and a new shower door and we did this for less than $1,500 dollars.

So who is fooling who mother is so gullible or just lying to me or she will believe anything my sister and brother in law will tell her, they even told mother she cannot spend any of her money and if she did mother would lose her medicate.

Ok anybody who knows anything about medicate knows is that you can spend your money as you see fit! If you want to go on a cruise around the world and spend $20,000 you can do it and medicate is not going to call you up and tell you that you cannot go on vacation and if you do we will take away your coverage!

Now of course my wife and I have gone to seminars with financial advisers with lawyers who told us the same thing that you can do what every you want with your money and send it were ever and on whatever you want to spend it on, and medicate will not and cannot take away your coverage.

But try to tell mother this, as the little respect mother has for me and any bit of respect for me and how she prescribes me with any bit of intelligent even when I tell mother I have gone to seminars with lawyers and financial advisers. The response I receive from her is always the same "NO, NO,

NO the law are different here in Georgia that is what the lawyer told me" right!! I said the law is the same across the United States and again I got the NO, NO, NO!!!

BUT!! Of course if mother want to buy a house then it was ok to purchase one so what is the difference in spending your money on a vacation or anything is different than buying a house and medicate is not going to take away your coverage.

How stupid does my mother think I am this was a ploy to get my mother's money into my sisters new home the down payment paid by mother and then change the will putting my sister as the recipient of the full value of the house if anything happened to mother and this would leave me out of anything left of my father's estate.

Which all of father estate that is left goes to my thieving sister and brother in law that carefully planned this farce to lure mother to move to Georgia and take all her money that half of it was left to me too.

So let me play this out for you and how all of this went down, first yes I wanted mother to either move in with me or my sister, and YES I want mother away from me to so I did not have to take care of her any more, for 20 years after father's death I was in charge of taking care of mother.

Where was my sister when all of this was going on well living in Georgia of course away from her did not lift a finger to help not one bit not even once. Of course she came running when mother was laid up with her knee replacement but that was for two weeks. I was doing everything else for weeks on end all the doctor appointments and shopping helping her to clean her house and do laundry which my wife helped.

My wife and I never had our hands out for anything never asked for anything and even never looked for anything even when I was out of work for 6 month and after two years out of work again for another 5 months. I worked a part time job and the wife had a job. Never heard my mother say poor!poor! Shawn out of work and having to work a part time bartending job to pay the bills and his wife having to work to help pay for things OH no never felt sorry for me!! Just felt sorry for my loser sister and her husband!

But I was the one making sure mother was not alone for any holidays, made sure she was invited to my house for every mother's day and birthdays, as well as my in laws, my children, my wife's and mine.

Ran over to her house to fix any problems replace light bulbs that burned out, replace batteries on any of her clocks and smoke alarms. Move furniture, bring her shopping for food and take her to her doctors! Yes all of this was ongoing every week and more so the older mother got, and she could not do things for herself like drive, but all I heard was I can drive!

Sure I said you cannot hear and you need a hearing aid which you will not purchase because you do not think you need one, and you hands are so arthritic you cannot even turn the key to start your car, mother even had her mechanic put on your key a piece of plastic so you can grab it like a handle to start the car. Plus your shoulders are also arthritic you cannot even do hand over hand turn and you walk the wheel to the point the car shakes so much I get sea sick.

So who is fooling who not me I said you cannot live alone you need one of us to take care of you live with me or your daughter. Yes this was an opportune time for my sister so swoop in and get her hands on everything.

When mother was selling her house she told my wife that when I sell the house I will split the money and give you (meaning me) and your sister the money from the sale of the house.

So when my sister got wind of this she put a stop to that fast, she filled my mother head with all these lies of Medicaid taking away your coverage if you spent or gave your money away and told mother that is what the lawyer said to my sister when she was at the closing of the house.

Of course we all know where that went right into my sister's pocket so where is this written Medicaid will take away your coverage if you spend all your money?? No where that's were!

So now mother is living with my sister and my mother told me that she is paying my sister $600 a month for expenses to cover the electric, water, food and other expenses. Really I said how much are you using of all of the utilities I said, in the summer in Chicago just the two of us do not use $600 in utilities a month I said.

I told mother with my mother in law living with us I said I am not asking a dime from her to pay for anything not any utilities bills or food. Unless there is something she wants herself and then she can pay for it I said my mother in law is living with us for free mom were does my sister get off changing you $600 a month to live with her!!

I am not as dumb as my mother thinks I am mother has slipped out information to my mother in law without her knowing it, mother has even said this. Mother told my mother in law you know that my sister business was not doing so well and they were not making a lot of money!

As is said earlier my sister is in deep debt and this is the only reason she would have taken mother to live with her to help my sister to pay off the debt of her franchise business or she will have to file bankruptcy for all the money she owes into that franchise company that is why and the only reason why my sister would want mother to live with her.

So my sister got my mother to move in with her to be her personal ATM machine! That is what my older son said she was an ATM machine he also said when grandma goes the ATM will be shut off and no more money will be coming out of it and all the money left to my sister and brother in law will not last very long and they will be back on the poor street.

Yes I said to him you are right and that will happen but why is it alright to screw me over, I was someone who never did anything wrong to my sister or mother but I was treated as a stupid person and abused by my mother and now my only sister who never acted like a sister!

I wanted my mother to move in with my sister and yes that is my fault but who would have guessed my sister would screw me over like that!! I should of known she would do something like that when she said to me one time "you are my little brother I would never screw you over I would never do that to you" SURE you wouldn't but you did! So one thing if you take anything away from reading this book is make sure you cover your ASS!!!

If someone tells you they will never do that to you, you can bet on it they will screw you over if given the chance so you should cover ASS yourself, make sure you do or this will happen to you as it will and can happen to anyone else it can happen to you.

Some time in life you learn the hard way, but I have also learn in life what goes around comes around, you do bad things bad things to family it will happen to you, bad karma will find you and bad things will happen to you three fold.

But this little boy has a few tricks up his sleeve, so I have been in contact with a Georgia lawyer which I will not tip my hand just yet, there will be a big surprise for them when mother passes you'll see.

They think this person who they thought was dumb because of learning disabilities cloud not do anything just wait!!

So be sure you do not do bad things to family members because family can bring to your life bad karma, and as an Italian I know a few things about bad karma such as the Malocchio better known as Maloik, this is where you do not what this in your life if you give someone the Malocchio you are wishing bad things to happen to them and they can and they will happen.

The Italian's believe that this word and many Italians believe in malocchio (often pronounced "maloik.") Part superstition, part tradition, it is the belief in the evil eye, placed on someone when someone else is jealous or envious of the other's good luck. The malocchio then manifests itself in some sort of misfortune onto the cursed person, usually some physical ailment or misfortune in everyday life, like losing a job and not able to find a new one things breaking down around the house or even car accidents.

There is something to be said about the Malocchio when an Italian puts the Malocchio on you it is a bad as a witch putting a spell on you. Just as bad and just as evil, some people do not believe in this, but I do as a full blooded Italian I believe in the Malocchio I believe in it so much I were a special necklace that protects me from this evil.

I have warn this necklace ever since my father died it was his and I took it from him on his death bed in the hospital as he was dying I removed from him and put it on and have never take it off and I have been wearing it ever since.

It has protected for this Malocchio and I do not say I have not had bad things happen to me and they have, I have lost my job twice in 5 years but I was able to find a new job with hard work and sticking to looking for a new job and not giving up, this is where I know this necklace has protected me and helping me find a new job, call it superstition call it what every you like my necklace works!! So if you ever want to know what this necklace is I will show you some day if you ask.

You can also go on line and type the word Malocchio you will get the definition of the word and information about this evil eye as they call it and you can see what my necklace looks like.

Chapter 5

Backing up to my childhood there are things that happen I think I will never know the truth about of what happened to me. I have been told one thing but as I try to re-enact certain accidents that supposed of happened to me and it does not make sense to me let me try to explain what I mean and you can come to your own conclusion.

I was only 24 months old as I was told when I lost the top part of my little pinky finger on my left hand and this was due to a 1950's push lawn mower because of playing with the large drive wheel of the lawn mower. As this was explained to me when I was older and listing to my mother tell everyone in the family this is how it went.

Mother said she had just finishing cutting the grass with this mower (ok first as far back as I can remember I have never known my mother to do any yard work, maybe I am wrong and I could very well be wrong but it does not add up to me). So mother said she had finished cutting the grass and then hung this mower on the wall OK!

First my mother even when she was in her younger years mother was not able to pick up this mower or even push this thing around the yard so how could I of played with this wheel on the wall when it was obviously on the ground and then move the wheel when it was on the ground and a child of 24 months even move this thing.

I must have played with the large wheel and turned it and my hand went across the blade and that was how I lost the top part of my finger plus almost losing the next two fingers which it is hard to believe because there are no scars on my other fingers just the top of my finger missing so how could I of almost lost them too with out and scars or even having any kind of circulation problems like I have with my little finger that is missing the top.

As stated early in this book father was working the night shift and sleeps during the day so mother said she was done and had hung the heavy mower on the wall, but when this happened I screamed and mother screamed so loud that father fell out of bed and came running into the back yard to see what had happened which I was rushed to the hospital.

But was left behind was the top of my finger which could have been saved and sowed back on?

To this day how it happened will be a mystery to me but the real truth is locked inside of my mind and as I was growing up there has been dreams of me standing in front of a window and looking down I could see a part of a finger on the window cell with blood and then I would wake up and I would try to remember what I just dreamed.

Some how I know I was trying to remember what really happened to my finger and my mind keeps bring it up but it is never complete and I know I will never know how this happened to me.

But in the 50's and thing like this was more like the stone age of medicine compared today doctors they could of saved my finger but not then, so in the hospital the doctors took a graph of skin from my knee to wrap around my finger and as you would expect mother told the doctor why did you not take it from his butt were it could not be seen.

As I said I will never know the really story of what happened that day just what I was told but it does not add up to me and will have to live with this now. I ask myself where was my sister when this was going on? Why was I outside when mother was doing such a dangers thing? And not in some kind of play pen funny I think.

There was another time as a child I think I was 5 years old and play cowboys and I think with my sister in the back yard and mom and dad were sitting on the porch, I remember playing and the next thing I knew I was getting rushed to the hospital again for putting my arm thru a glass screen door cutting under my arm needing a number of stitches and again as I was told that I ran up to the door and put my arm thru it with my toy gun.

OK that does not make sense to me either how playing in the back ended up putting my arm thru a glass door was I pushed? I do not know and I know I will never know the truth to anything that happened.

As I explain before mother never like to lessen to me or want to hear anything I had to say about anything I was wrong about anything and everything.

I have a perfect example to prove my point, there was one time I was riding my bike with my friends, yah amazing I had friends not many but a few. So one of my friends drove up one of the neighbors new driveway you know fresh laid concrete well it was dry and he did not leave any marks so the neighbor comes out and started yelling at my friend telling him to get off the driveway.

So he goes over to his parent's house to let the parent's know what their son had done and of course I was there and got blamed for the same thing. Of course mother started yelling at me about doing that I said I was no were near the driveway or even rode my bike on it.

What do you think mother would not believe me or even want to hear anything about it I was guilty by association and no matter how much I cried and said I did not do anything wrong she would not hear of it I had to go over to the neighbors house and apologize. I was crying so hard I could not even say the words I was sorry for riding on his driveway.

All mother would say did you see the look on his face he knew he was wrong to accuse you of doing something he knew you did not ride on his driveway. WHAT! Yes WHAT! The hell, mother knew I was not guilty and would not back me up and make me apologize for something I did not do.

How damaging is that to a child, you did nothing wrong and you get blamed for something you did not do, and your own parent would not believe their own child how much does that damage a child trust in their own parent.

There are so many times were things happen that I was blamed for that I did not do or was even there I got in trouble for it, and trying to explain that to mother and her high pitched screaming and yelling blaming me for something I never did.

To this day I remember some of the things I was blamed for I did not do and was punished for, there is an anger still inside and were my anger will never go away or have any closer to what I have learned to live with and just forget it.

I made had a promises to myself that I would never ever be that way to my children and when I had my own children and they were old enough we had a very nice talk.

I made it very clear to my sons that could come to me with anything and I would not raise my voice or even get made or ever judge them or take anyone side of who did what and who was to blame until I knew and had all the information before we worked out the problem and made sure we had a solution to it.

There were many times not too many times my sons had some issues that we could not fix or come to an agreement on how to take care of it. There was one time my oldest son was being bulled and we talked about getting into fights and I told him under no circumstance do you start a fight and you only get into a fight unless it is self defense and even then you warn that person what will happen if you do not stop.

From what I was told my son was being pushed around by the other child bulling him and my son said he warned him three times of what he would do if this person did not stop what he was doing and upon the third warning this child and he did not stop and on the fourth attempt of pushing him my son put one right on his nose this stopped this bully right in his tracks and he started to cry and my son said I warned you three times to leave me alone.

I was told about this when my son came home and I was not made and he knew that he was not going to get into trouble with me and that I would back him up if this child's parents came to me about this issue.

Well of course they did and they did which I told them my son had warned their child to leave him alone and my son's retaliation was in self defense and my son was not going to apologue for his actions that there child should apologize for his actions.

As things came together my son and that other child became friends, I feel this is how parents should be a role model to their own children, no not to fight with others but to let them know that they can to come to you with any problem they have and to have an open line of communications, never make your child be afraid to tell you anything it is so healthy for a parent to have an open relationship with their children.

If more parents would have this type of relationship with their children there would be less problem children in the US today, and you ask how come I was not a problem child because of the non communications with my mother, well I had my father we could talk about anything and he would just lessen and give me his opinion, my father was a great inspiration to me and I hope I am that way with my son's.

Of course dad had other ways of getting his point across to me like when I got my driver's license he said one thing to me "NO SPEEDING" and all I said was yes dad, and the best one was when I was old enough to drink dad's best line as "NO DRIVING DRUNK". When you get these commands from a very firm Italian father you either do what they say or you will pay for your actions BIG time.

I followed my father's rule with my own son's and when my son's were old enough to drink I had one simple rule, if you had too much to drink I do not want you to drive call me any time of day or night and I promises I will never be mad and I will come and get you and not give you a lecture or yell at you.

There was one time my oldest son 18 at the time used my cab service one night over the summer I was in bed sleeping and about 1:00 am our phone rings and on the other side was my oldest calling said dad I need to be picked up without asking him any reason I said were are you.

He said sheepishly the Bartlet police department?? OK I said I will be right there so the wife and I jumped into my car and picked him up, he was waiting outside and he jumping to the car and I asked do I need to go into the police department for any reason he said no we can go.

Then my son started to explain why he was in the police department first he said someone else was driving and he had not done any drinking and the reason they were in the Bartlet police department they were pull over because the officer saw a car full of kids driving around late at night.

Found a car full of underage kids under the influence but no one was arrested but all the kids had to call their parents and they had to be pickup. I could see the look on my son's face that he was worried I was going to punishes him or start yelling at him, I just comely said I was not mad and happy you had a designated driver and you were not driving. Then I ask where is your car at, he said it was at his friend's house and that he was going to get it in the morning,

I then said great no problem and I said nothing for the rest of the ride home but my son was telling us about the party and what was going on.

The reason I talk about this is because as parents we need to keep that line of commutation open with our children which is very, very important because if my son was afraid of what I would do finding him drunk who knows what could of happened?

The only open line of communications I had was with my father and never ever had any kind of communications with my mother, I could never sit down and have a normal conversation with mother or even tried to for one thing I was not going to get any kind of answer or constructive feedback so why bother. I had better conversations with my friends and coworkers then I ever could with my mother.

If that was me and she got that phone call who knows what would have happened to me or I would have been left at the police department to rot for all I know, but father would of come for me and he would of not said much just give me one of his looks so I know that I was smart enough not to drive.

I push this for parents make sure you can communicate with your children let them know they are never too old to confide in you and be a friend to them someone they can come to and tell you anything and not be afraid to talk to you.

Because if you do not who are they talking to who knows who they will talk to, and do what your child talking to a stranger and will they tell what is right thing to do, you want your child to come to you with a problem instead of someone else that could give them the wrong advise.

I do not clam to be an expert on how to raise children but I think I have done a really good job with my own and I hope they do that with their own children some day.

Recognition, now there is a word in the English language that really carries weight, how I would love to have just a little bit of that word in my life I know with someone giving a little bit of recognition would of changed my life for the better.

As I touched on this word earlier in this book I have no idea what that feels like having been recognized for what I have accomplished and have done in my life.

I would like to get into this more, this word recognition and which it goes hand in hand with praise, wow just thinking of these two words makes me feel good and I want to do something to receive recognition and praise.

But growing up without these words is something very hard to deal with not having even praise makes my eyes start to water, I look for that, I want to hear it! I know this is why when I do something I go all in and give it everything I have to succeed and finish on top above everyone.

Which everyone knows that does not happen all the time and I get crushed when I do not finish first, but I am happy that I gave it my all and give myself my own recognition and a pat on the back for a job well done.

I stated confidence is something I do not have but I go and force myself to do things and trying new things to build confidence in myself. Even to this day I still have to force myself to do something out of my comfort zone. Playing golf is a self improving sport and which has given me a great deal of confidence in myself and the challenge it brings when you play this sport by yourself, yes you play golf with a few friends but it is you against your friends who is going to have the lower score.

So try playing golf in a tournament you will learn a lot about yourself fast, because golf is not a team sport where you can rely on others to help you win. You are on your own with no support but your own self and someone like me who was raised without confidence or support you will get run over and eaten alive.

So when I saw this tournament at a golf show called the Mesquite amateur I took home the DVD and said to my wife I want to try this it looks like a lot of fun. I was excited to try something like this for amateurs you play with other with your same skill level.

But never have played in a tournament before and this is very difficult especially for someone like me but I wanted to give it a try, so I had to wait a hole year because we had already set our vacation and this tournament was the same time.

When the following year came around I signed up and could not wait for the end of May to arrive to play in this tournament. We arrive in Las Vegas one day for the tournament and we drove to Mesquite which was just a one hour drive out side of Las Vegas, we checked into our hotel then headed to the registration location checked in and then got ready to get up early to find my way to the first golf course.

Finding the first golf course and it was just like what the pro's do you check in and get your official score card and get warmed up at the rang then wait for the call to get to your carts and head to your first hold. I had so many butterflies in my stomach when they made the call and we drove to my first hole and get ready to tee off.

Let me tell you how nervous I was when it was my turn to tee off as I address the ball my hands started to shake and looked down the fairway and all I could see was a large wash on the left side and a small mountain on the right side of the fair way with a bunker almost in the middle of the fairway and all I could think of how the heck do I do this!

I was so afraid of where was this ball was going when I hit it, with my confidence level falling and wounding way am I doing this and wanted to run and give up, I started to calm myself down by telling myself you can do this it is just like any other golf course you play except for the large wash on the left and a mountain on the right, I took a deep breath and took my swing and hit this bullet right up the middle of the fairway right past the bunker in the fairway.

All I had left was just over a hundred yards to the green I pitch it to within about 20 feet of the hole and then three putted for a bogy. Great start I thought to myself dummy you go from a look at birdie to bogy but I was happy with myself I did it the start was not a disaster it was a ok start.

What would father say? I know what he would tell me what are you doing!! With his patented glare, I you know better than to leave a birdie putt short!! But this set the pace for me placing smart shots with a chance for par or even birdie only had one bird all day but at the end of the round I shooting an 83 and for me never playing at course or what to expect in the desert I was 5 strokes under my handicap and for that course my handicap was 16.

Well by the of the first round I was tied for first on the second day still played well and by the third and final round I was still playing well but not sure how I finish in my division of players that have the same handicap as me, so I had to wait for after dinner when the scores were posted.

So had to eat dinner and wait, but really was too nervous to eat when you did not know if you made the cut to play in the championship round the next day so when the scores were posted of that day I saw that I came in 4th place the feeling of accomplishment was so over whelming I was staring to cry but had to hold it in because I think it was a little childish to show that kind of emotion for something like this.

My wife told me she was so proud of me I was so excited and could not wait for tomorrow to see how I would do up agents the rest of the field. Well the bubble burst by the end of the day did not play real well but gave it a good effort and ended up somewhere in the middle of the field.

This event was so much fun and have meet some great guys and made some long time friends and look forward to this tournament every year. I keep coming back year after year and I have been doing this tournament for 10 straight years now and plan on doing it every year I can,

I have gotten involved with other players for the past two years we have been raising money for scholarships for local children to give back to the community and we have given out scholarships money to help high school grads with some money for college. We have get donations for golf equipment and rounds of golf which we sell tickets to raffle off the prizes and I am in charge of sell raffle tickets and for someone who has not a lot of confidence this is a tall order but as I pointed out I work very hard at not being that way anymore and takes a lot of effort to be a better person with my shy tendency I need to be outgoing and selling thickets.

But I look at it this way I am doing something good for someone else and it is very rewarding for me to do this and is not hard to get out there and be yourself and to do good for others.

Meeting these other players who got me involved I have made more friends that I know will last a long time also they make me feel good about myself and they are good friends who trust me to do a good job for the scholarship fund.

As I said I have been going to this golf tournament for 10 years now and in 2009 I finished first place in my division winning by one stroke. Our first round was at a new course that opened up for the first time the course was called Coyote Springs and it was a very windy and hot day.

Talk about being scared and nervous, OK I know you are saying why is he so nervous something he has done before what is the big deal right, remember I have no confidence in myself I get this way every year I play because I want to do well and prove to myself I can do this, it has be an uphill battle my whole life even at this age not getting any confidence or support growing up as a child stays with you all the time.

So back to playing this course for the first time as I said very nervous not knowing what to expect and how would I score but I keep thinking to myself everyone else has to play this course and the conditions too.

When we finished I added up my score and I shot an 88 which I was very mad at myself wondering where I placed in my division, so as I was talking to all the other players I was hearing scores in the mid to upper 90's so I was felling not to bad of how I would be in the standings. After dinner that night I got the scores sheets and saw I was in second place two strokes behind the first place guy.

Wow I thought to myself I did pretty well considering the conditions so on the second day we play a more familiar course and I was pared with the top 3 players, my score on the second day was even better with an 83 which put me in first place by 3 strokes.

On the final day we played one of my more favorite courses called The Palms first hole was a par 3 over a valley well my tee shot found the bunker to the right of the green and from there it went down hill almost put my bunker shot out of bounds and then got it to the green then 4 putted for a 7 which put be 3 strokes behind everyone else.

At that point I thought I was done but I gather myself and though of my father of what he would have told me if he was there and dad would of said that is one hole you have 17 more to go just stay with it and play your game.

Calming myself down our next tee shot was from a elevated tee 100 feet to the fair way below took a deep breath and hit a perfect drive to the middle of the fair way from there I pared the hole and took that and built and good round shooting of an 87 that was good enough to win my division by one stroke.

The reason why I put this in my book is to show reads that anything is possible when you put your mind to what you want, never give up or give in to your own short comings. This is a lot coming from someone with no self confidant's or self worth, playing golf torments has given me a lot of self confident's specially in what I do every day this is why parents you need to give your children all the self confidants you can your children look up to you and need self worth and most of all self confidents.

As a child growing up I never had any kind of self worth or a pat on the back for a job well done being pushed a side as a child not worth anything I grow up not feeling I had any self worth or encouragement that you can do anything you put your mind to.

This is what I had to do all my life, pushing myself to do better be the best I can be in life, at a job and even playing golf or any sport I want to play as a child and now as an adult.

My sons have been given all the praise I could give them in anything they did, playing sports in there jobs and in school they never stopped getting encouragement from me or my wife that is why they are so successful today.

I am so proud of my sons they are so successful today because we put encouragement and praise into there lives making them to be the best they can be at anything they do.

My oldest son is a professional licensed land surveyor he continues going to school to get more licenses and degrees, were my youngest son went on to college got his degree in culinary arts and is now an executive chief and director which we could not be any more proud of them.

See parents just giving your children support, praise and encouragement gives them the confidents to do what ever they are passionate in doing and they also have learned that life does not give you anything, you will fall down you will fail but you need to get back up more and more determined to succeeded of what you want in life.

If I would of be given some support, praise and encouragement who knows were I could be today, I could have been someone special maybe a VP of purchasing or even a professional golfer, all I had to do was have a little confidences in myself I could of taken my fathers offer to go to that golf school and learned to play golf at a professional level.

But without any support or confidence I had no desire to go to golf school, but if I had that opportunity today with my own built self confidence that offer of going to golf school there would of not been a second though of going and putting in a 100% effort of achieving what I wanted, and knowing that with the fight I have in my heart failing and getting back up and fighting for a dream and what I wanted who knows were I could be today.

Parents give your child all the positive support you can and all the encouragement there is, who knows what your child can achieve in life. If parents today would spend time with there children being a parent there would be less children getting into trouble and joining gangs and this country would have a whole lot less street violence.

As a parent myself I got into teaching and coaching baseball watching other coaches I was appalled of what I saw, yelling a screaming at kids not playing well or making mistakes children of a young age will make mistakes but that is how they learn to play the game.

My sons were not the best at the game but putting them in that sport they learn how to be a team player and sport others on there team. I could not stand other coaches of how they were teaching that sport so I got involved.

As a coach myself I made the game fun to play giving the lesser skilled children an opportunity to play other positions they wanted to play I could see the joy of playing baseball fun again, it is not about winning but what you do to contribute to the team and contribute to a win that maters.

As a coach for 4 years my teams had fun playing and I would select kids who I coached before, our league had draft day and all the coaches would get together and select players from the past year. I know some coaches would select the best players so they could put together a team that would with the championship.

These coaches were that self absorbed and wanted to be a coach to have the best team to win it all and all they though of winning and nothing else, how shallow how about the kids it is all about them and not just winning that is what baseball is all about team work and playing together and having fun.

As a coach my kids had fun when I had kids I coached before and they were on my team they would say oh boy I am on Mr. Woods team that is great. Do you know how that made me feel, it was so heart warming to hear that from them and I did not let me down.

Coaching kids and developing there minds on how to be a team player and being a better person I know I made a difference to a lot of kids. Some of my coaching techniques were posting the line up sheet with there statistics on it, I could here the joy of them saying I am batting this percentage and look I was getting better at hitting, positive reinforcement is the best way to coach a child in anything.

I went as far as giving every kid on my team a nick name which they loved and I even called them that nick name, there was on child on my team who I selected every year and he played hard for me and the team, he would get hurt or make a really good play I gave him the nick name "the rock".

This child love that nick name I called him "the rock" every time he was on the field I would yell out nice play rock or great him rock I know he enjoyed being on my team and I know the parents were happy with me because they would come up to me and say my son was so happy that he was on my team.

At the end of each season I would take photos of each child in a baseball pose and surprise them with there own baseball card on the back I would have there position they played and batting average pitching stats.

Every year these kids would love there own baseball card and parents would say to me there child had so much fun play ball with me and that I was there coach and they were very happy with me on how I thought there child how to play baseball and be a team player.

A number of years later I ran into one of my boys that I coached it was at a event that I was bartending at the Indian Lakes county club that I bartended for over 26 years. Well it took me a minute to figure who it was and it was the boy I call the rock and I said to him how are you rock how are your parents are they doing well and how have you been.

Will this boy introduce me to his girl friend that he was engaged then he proceeded to tell her who I was and how grateful he was to me of all the years of coaching him in baseball and then he said that he had kept everyone of the baseball cards I had made for him over the years of coaching.

I can not put into words of how that made me feel I know that I had something to do with making this child growing into a man and I could tell he was a well respected person and that I had a small part of being a small influence on his life, but I know his parents are good people and they raised a great person.

Telling these things about my life is very important to me to share my experience with others maybe to make them better parents or to think of ways to be better parents and make there children better as they grow up.

Because I do not want other children to go thru life having this kind of abuse or any other kind of abuse, because our children are a blessing from a greater being and they should be cherished like the blessing they are with all the support, encouragement and love that we can give them.

Our children should grow up with the mindset that they can do anything they want as long as they put their mind to it, plus we have to know everyone has limitations and not everyone can be a rocket scientists or a doctor so this is where parents need to encourage their children to go on a different path.

Find something your child is passionate in and let our children run with it you will be surprised how they will succeed. To make a point my youngest son had his issues in school like I did, but he got so interested in cooking my wife put him in cooking classes in our park district which he loved and in high school he took all the home economics he wanted and when there was nothing else he could take.

We found that our high school offered cooking classes thru our Junior college technical school and they would bus the kids interested in becoming a chief, so he went there and really excelled I knew he had found his calling and when a culinary college came in to the Junior tech school and talked to the students.

He came home told us all about the college and said he wanted to go to this University and learn to be a chief he then told about all these other famous chief who went there, well he did not have to sell me on this opportunity, I know what he wanted and I encouraged him to go and apply and see if he would get accepted.

Well that did not take long with some of the letters his teachers wrote about him made it easy for him to get accepted, the wife and I went down to the University and we could see how excited he was and how much he wanted to go, so his journey began and as I said before he exceeded all expectation graduated and how is a executive chief and director.

But the road was not easy which is not always easy for everyone he had work harder than most and had his issues and at one point his major was nutrition and he found it harder then he thought and he could not be creative with his cooking as he liked to so he called me and we talked about it.

I had told him may times anything can be fixed if we work thru it to find a solution to his problem, and it was simple change your major back to Culinary arts and see what class will transfer to this major and what you will need to take for your new major.

We worked it out and he when to his counselor and got his classes changed and he found that he had to take a couple of classes to make up what he needed to change his major but he still was able to graduated on time.

This is what I preach all the time is leave an open line of communication with your children and never ever let them be afraid to come to you with anything because if you do not who knows what can happen. If I did not have that open line and was afraid to talk to me my son could have stayed on his path and fail and or even worst flunked out of Culinary College and were would he be now.

I am not taking credit for this but having that open line of communication I believe helped him make the right choice and to this day my sons can always talk to me.

One thing I hope is they have that same open communication with their children make that open line and keep it open I can see it with their children now but it is early yet and I hope they develop one as early as possible which I know there will be some nudging on my part to develop one.

Something I wish I had that with my parents an open line of communication, I had a good one with father but only to a degree he could understand what it was about it about most things but there are some things you just do not talk to you dad about and you need a mother to talk to but we all know where that was! There was nothing I could talk to mother about just had to figure it out by myself which there was a lot of hit or missed and learn by my mistakes when there were problems.

Most things in life and growing up it was on my own all alone with no one to turn to or talk to most of the time but either way a child should never feel alone with no one there to go to or help, that is the most loneliest feeling any one could have and I know it all too well it is like walking into a large auditorium and you are the only one there left alone with your thoughts.

That is a scary place for a child not as much for adults because they had other adults to talk to and possibly help which as I was grow up to an adult I had friends to talk to and get some guidance's that was it I said this before no mother to go to and tell her what is bothering me or even help.

But children on the other hand need guidance they need someone to talk to and were they can feel save doing so without any repercussion from their problems or issues.

Because without this kind of help and support for our children they our left along and will cling to the first person or persons they can talk to someone who will lessen and at very young age.

Our children are very impressionable this is where we lose our children they go to others get the wrong advise or the wrong direction other people can lead your child in the wrong direction or even the wrong path and they can start getting into trouble.

This is where bullying can start getting aggressive being told the wrong thing to do when have problems, lashing out at other adults and other kids that are smarter than them or more well adjusted finding ways to hurt others mentally as well as physical.

Because they themselves are hurting inside and do not know how to handle that feeling or even handle the felling of hurting, being frustrated and upset not knowing where to turn or who to talk to.

I think I was lucky I had good friends to talk to and who would just sit there and lessen to me vent and go on and on about my issues and problems. They were good sometimes they even helped and helped me work thru my problems with college and even girls. Even to this day I am still friends with most of them today my friends came from good back grounds themselves and was lucky to meet them and became friends for life.

Children need good friends it is the parent responsibility to get their children involved with other kids just like them with morals and habits developing good scholastic skills. This can help your children with school and growing even help them to get along with others to develop leader ship skills and team work.

Parents I do not claim to be all knowing on how to raise children but I think I have something over others they do not know about as just a few simple words or a helping hand can go a long way with children.

Being a coach in baseball was very rewarding for me I leaned so much from all these kids I learned that how flexible children are and understanding when you work with them and make what they do fun and a learning experience they absorbed everything so fast and learn so easily.

That is something I could have used growing up and going thru school myself I learned it almost too late but there was that college professor who gave me the right tools on how to study which helped me get thru college and graduate I will forever be grateful for his help and guidance.

If only I learned this earlier in my life going thru school I could have been a better student with better grades without my struggles and problems that followed me thru my early years.

My parents could have learned this method of helping learn how to read especially my mother she could have made learning fun and a happy experience not one of yelling and screaming and making me cry all the time.

That is why today reading is not my most favorite thing in the world to do; I have to force myself to read anything like emails office memos, letters and contracts for my job, I wonder how I can do anything in life that involves reading and writing these things are such a chore for me because I have to work at it.

Sometimes I think it holds me back from really excelling at the job I do because I am really good at what I do for a living I learned to go from assistant manager retail store to purchasing to senior purchasing agent and now purchasing manager.

Where would I be today if I had the skills of reading and spelling of a adult not of a 6th or 8th grader as you can tell by reading this book that has been written by me.

Even having the confidence in myself to go out and explore new things or try something I have never done before were could I be or what changes in my life even how my life could have been better but I will never know?

As I said earlier in my book father wanted to send to golf school to learn how to play golf at a competitive level who knows were or what could have happened today? I could have been on the PGA tour or somewhere in the golf world doing something good in my life for other people, maybe even teaching golf to the younger players or even guiding children to a sport that build character in them and make them a better person, my life could be a whole world different if I was given that chance.

What I mean by this is given the support, understanding, guidance and love to help your children make the right choices and head them into the right directions. Yes mistakes happen and the wrong choices are made but if they have the support and help of the parents anything is possible.

Chapter 6

———

To this day my mother still does not respect me or even tell me the truth about anything, at over 60 years old I am insulted, belittled, emasculated, embarrassed and mentally abused.

Nothing has changed from growing up till now I believe my mother could not tell the truth or even be nice to me if she tried everything she does it to beat me down and try to make me feel worth less.

Now family members and cousins will tell me I am lying and just wrong, but I am not exaggerating or lying no one will believe me on what I have written in this book but all have to say to my cousins is, you have to live with her to fully understand what I am saying. First of all they never lived with mother or had her get mad at you for something you did or did do in my case.

But there have been a few cousins by marriage in to our family who have seen mother for her real self and know how she is because they have experienced it themselves.

So here is a perfect example of how she is, I cannot remember the occasion were we had all of the Wood's over for a Barbeque party and one of my cousins was still going to college and wanted some time to do reading and to get away from all the noise so he borrowed my room.

No big deal right!! Will not so in mother's eye my cousin used my bed to lie down and read, ok still no big deal but my new confider was still on the bed and you say ok so, but not with mother after the party she questioned me about and asked who was on my bed and I did not know anything thing but said our cousin wanted to do some reading and get away from everybody I told him to use my room if he wanted to do some reading.

Thinking he would use my desk I said well mother goes off on the deep end and started yelling a screaming he put his greasy head on the pillows of the confider and could of stained them with all the grease he puts in his hair, now remember this was back in the 60's and guys would put stuff on their hair to keep it in place.

But no one heard this but us and not our cousin why because this was mother favorite person and his mother was my ant Rose which was mothers favorite, anyone else like one of my friends or other family members that was not on her favorite list she would of jumped all over them.

Not enough for you I have many examples how about this one were someone on the Wood side of the family really got the full fury of mother and mother got it back this was a thing of beauty.

This was about 5 years ago one of our cousin was getting married and this was at the reception dinner so we were sitting at the dinner table about 10 of us it was me and the wife two of my cousins children and their mother Sue, along with my mother and four other Wood's family members.

We will call my cousin Jack for this encounter that he was starting college and had grown a beard and his hair was a bit long, whatever the wife and I like the look but of course mother does not like any mail with facile hair and long hair as well.

Because mother never let me along when it came to how I looked as to how I grew my own hair and facile hair, she would always be on my case of why my hair is too long or why did I grow a mustache and she did not like my goatee always getting on me about that and then when I got older on how I was losing my hair and why is it going gray and on top of that what is should do to stop it from falling out and what to take or use.

I believe these were things mother like using on me to make me feel inferior every time I would see mother it was never "I son how are you and you are looking good how are things you feeling good" No it was always why are you going bald I do not like your mustache and goatee I makes you look dirty! Or it would be your getting fat and your belly is sticking out.

You can see why I never wanted to be around her and even see her because of these types of insults or belittling every time I would see her or when I would come over to the house to fix something or repair whatever needing fixing after father passed.

So let me get back to poor Jack so we are sitting at the table having fun talking about college with my cousin and just having a good time, until mother started on Jack.

She started to bagger him about the way he looked first she started out with, Jack why is your hair so long it makes you look dirty!

Jack why do you not shave your beard you look like a hippy!

Jack your long hair and beard makes you look like a bum!

Well that was all Joan, Jacks mother could take she told my mother to shut up and leave her son alone and said if Jack wants to grow his hair along and have a beard that is his business and you can keep your comments to yourself and if Jack wants to express himself, why he grows his hair and beard that is his business and his along.

There was not a sound out of our table, mother had nothing to say my wife and I just looked at each other and smiled of course I wanted to stand up and applaud what Joan said but it was about time someone else had experienced mother's wrath regarding your taste in facile hair and length of one's hair.

I turned to Joan and said that is what I have been dealing with all my life always getting picked on the way my hair looked no one can express themselves with mother having to put in her two cents worth. Only one thing that would have made it perfect would be mothers favorite cousin were able to hear mother that does not do anything wrong and get to see that Joan just put her in her place like she did to mother.

Then a litter later mother started to complain that her neck was bothering her and she was not feeling good! Well of course mother you just got told off and you do not like that Hu! Someone you cannot bully or push around what a shame.

Mother came with my wife and I and we were not about to leave the wedding just because you were not feeling good because you were put in your place, how does that feel mother, not so good dose it!!

As you can tell my mother has favoritism to certain people like my sister and brother in law they can do no wrong everything is ok with them mother never picked on anything my sister does not even when she does not were makeup and mother is big on that when my wife is not wearing any makeup or does not like how she has it on well mother will give you direction on how it should look and how to put it on.

My sister never wears any makeup but mother will never say anything to her about how she looks and why you never put any makeup on. Sure this is the same way with other people, family, friends, relatives and cousins there are some they can do no wrong and there are some mother will always say something derogatory to them no matter what they do she will not like anything they do or say.

There was another incident with a family member his name is Jay there was a time he would do anything for mother pick her up take her to the doctors or even shopping but there was a time I do not know what happen I think mother went off on him and they go into it. I wish I was there to see it but my never know the next time I see him I will have to ask about that.

So if you are not one of mother favorite people you will always get picked on and abused when some people hear mother go off on other people I do not think they get it and they would be standing right there with me when mother would go off on something about me or how I looked but somehow my family and cousins would think it was funny or just that how you mother is!

No I would say try living with that all you life and tell me how does that feel never to have a kind word our support on what you want to do with your life just derogatory comments all the time, yelling and screaming at you for everything and anything if you make a mess getting her precious stove dirty or leave dishes in the sink.

I would tell my cousins I lived my whole life this way and you never had to go thru what I have had to endure, you had love support from your parents.

But as I said before none of my cousins would believe what I want thru or even believe what I am writing is true they never saw the real mother only I did she was never supportive or understanding even someone you could just sit and talk to about any of your problems or issues even a friendly conversation about just the weather.

This was something she never would want to sit and just lessen to you and my cousins never had that problem I know they could sit with their parents and talk about anything and are able to express themselves and have a understanding parent.

Watching TV and seeing all of these singing shows or other type of reality TV were the mothers say how proud of their child trying to live their dream and the support they would get for one or both parents telling how they supported their child wanting to work hard and go after their dream of what every they wanted to do without insults or derogatory comments of you cannot try that or you are not good enough to try that!

With that in mind I found ways of staying away from mother while I still lived at home, yes I have been asked you could of moved out when you were 21 and I said yes I could of moved out but working part time and trying to go to college at the same time I could not afforded that and I was going to graduate college at any cost just so I could prove a point to my mother that I could do something without anyone's help or support.

I never had any support from mother and dad was supportive the best he could but it was very, very hard to live this way so the older I got the more I was out of the house and out of mother way so when I started college I would be out of the house by 6:00 am going to class then after class I would head to my part time job work until 10:00pm and head home mother would be at work and dad would be watching TV, I would grab the left over dinner and head to my room to study. Then start this routine all over again all week long and on weekends I would be at my part time job working then going out with friends or on dates again just burring the candle at both ends as I stated earlier in this book which kept me out of the house.

Sunday would be a day to sleep in a little see mom for an hour or two until she went off to work and I would then spend my time studding or watching TV with dad and we would make dinner together watch sports all day and night, those are the times I miss the most of being with my dad just hanging around and doing things we like together I miss our time and I miss dad very much.

As I said before dad was a man of few words we got along so well we did a lot together not as much as some sons and dads would do but we did a lot more with more quality time then others kids and their dads would do.

But cherishing the time we spend with dad was the best time I ever had, my wife knows about these days because when we were dating she would come over and have dinner with us weather it was Saturday hamburger day or Sunday spaghetti it was always the best time and even my wife has said many times how she misses those days.

Dad would go to his garden and pick fresh tomatoes, peppers and beets to make with hamburger day and spaghetti Sunday, I know my wife understands why I like these days of the week and I would make sure with our children we would have dinner together as much as we could.

Having dinner as a family I feel is very important for the structure of an family this is where everyone can come together and talk about their day and parents can lessen to their children and be there for problems and just have a closer bond between each other this is so healthy for families to do more of because I know this is a dyeing family trait.

Our family rarely had dinner time together it was dad had left for his grave yard shift and I was eating with my sister with mom or after started working regular hours it was dad having dinner with us and mom was off working.

Either the case we hardly sat at the dinner table together some weekends we would have dinner as a family some holidays we had family dinner together but as a family no dinner was not much of a together place of course when my sister got married at 19 and was out of the house that ended any dinner time as a family.

But that is why in my family we would have many dinners together yes there were times as the kids got older and with after school activities that did not always happen but we made every effort to sit and have our dinner together as much as possible.

Being a father myself I thought it would be very hard and yes at times it was I learned a lot from my dad on how to be a good father and the most important thing to be a good father is to listen to your children and if you are a good listener you can hear a lot what they are saying and your children will be more willing to talk to you about anything of their issues if the parent would just listens to them.

When you can be that type of parent your children will just open up to you about anything and they will want your advice and your help. There were so many times and even to this day my sons will come to me and just want to talk and I love that I just want to be there for them and just be a dad.

A uncaring parent will jump all over you for something you did wrong or unsupportive and that is where we as parents fail and our children do not want to talk with us and this is where we loss them and they go off and get advice from someone else, and is this what we really want for our children going to someone else and not to us.

So much of this is our fault as parents we are too busy to listen to them do not have the time to just sit and listen. This is very important to them especially at a young age when they look up to you as a parent and want your help or support because we are there for them and they need us.

I said earlier my dad and I would just sit around and watch TV, mostly sports as you would guess golf or whatever the season was that's what we would do. Well I did that with my sons too what every they were watching I would be on the floor with them Saturday afternoon cartoons or evening shows that they like to watch I would be on the floor with them just being with them this was such a special time for us to bond and a family.

There was one night after dinner they were down stairs watching TV and my oldest son yelled out to me and side "hey dad The Three Stooges are on" of course I loved the Stooges so I ran down stars and got on the floor with them to watch our favorite show.

Just so you all know for many years I would be with my son's watching TV on the floor after dinner and of course after their home work was done being with them bonding.

Now remember the Stooges were from the 50's and this was the early 90's, but well call me a bad parent I let them watch the Stooges and they loved these guys and they love watching them and so did I we would laugh all the time, but of course my son's new this was all acting and what they did was not real and they know that would really hurt if you got hit with a hammer.

"Hey they made it thru life without being some kind of crazy person".

These are some good memories of me being with my sons and a father that I will never forget.

When my oldest purchased his own home and the youngest went off to college, I could not go down stairs and watch TV any more without them because I missed them so much and it felt lonely without them and I could not be in that room, so I would just watch TV in our sitting room which I did for many years before I could go back down stairs. As a father I am so close to my son's like I was with my father I feel it is very important that mothers and fathers have close bonding relationships with your children which I never had any kind of close bond with my mother just my father because of the things we did together it can be simple things like making dinner watching sports or even playing golf together.

I developed a close bond with my sons because we like to do a lot of same things together as I said earlier, but one thing I feel gave us the best bond in the world to us was camping together my good friend Jerry and I went camping with my sons when they were 10 and 5 years old, it was some of the most fun a father could do with his children, and when you start incorporating there friends it was even more special because it looked to me as more then a father but a friend to have fun with.

Well we did the camping thing for a total of 19 years we missed the last 3 years but will try to keep it up when we can have time to do it, it gets harder now because of my sons have family and kids of there own.

I remember our first camping trip as if it was last week and they do to when we get together with there now Uncle Jerry we talk about it. There was one trip we were sleeping in our tent and a storm was coming up and started to get windy I said let me get the chairs and garbage and put it away so I got up to go out of the tent and saw something in the garbage. You learn early not to leave a garbage bag on the ground so we peaked our heads out of the tent like "The Three Stooges" and then saw the largest black and white tale of a skunk back out of the garbage bag it was the biggest skunk I have ever seen.

My youngest said what do we do dad what do we do! All I said was what ever the skunk wants to do we are not going out of this tent once the skunk left I jump out of the tent and put the garbage bag in the car and got back in the tent.

We have had so many memorable camping trips I could be there for hundreds of pages telling you about them, and I know because of doing things like this together we are so close no one can understand.

But the point I am trying to make is our children need us to be open parents loving non forceful but guiding and helping, if more parents are like this our children would be more successful as adults less crime and better humans and this could better world for all of us.

So you may say how did I turn our so good or why I was not a troubled child getting into trouble, well I had a very good father figure to follow and I had good friends to help guide me to understand why you should be a better person and I thank my friends for being there for me when I need them the most and a father who was there for me as a mentor to me and someone I could look up to as a good person of society dad worked hard for his family and never complained.

It is never to late for parents to start to open those lines of communication and to be a good leister let your children know you will be there for them and help them thru there problems in life with out any repercussions plus there is no problem to big that you can not work out together as parents, we need to be a role models and someone they can look up to.

My sons have always look at the way my wife and I have work very hard for everything we have and we have good ethics and worked hard to have a good living for them. We have worked part time jobs to bring in extra money so we could have the better things in life and be able to have nice vacations.

We never had to rely on anyone for anything never had to call up either parents and cry about not having enough money to buy grocers or clothes because of our own ability to stand on our own two feet even when I was laid off from work for months on end, the wife work and I keep my part time job to supplement what unemployment was not giving us.

I am not saying we were perfect parents but our first year of marriage like anyone else was hard especially buying our first house having car repair issues and the cost we could not afford at first, yes mother took the car and help with the repairs which help greatly but mother did not have to rub it in our faces telling people who great she was for doing this and this type of behavior really caused issues.

Mother would never rub it in my sister's face how she would take my nephews out for haircuts and buy them clothes for school and school supplies, because my sister and brother in-law could not afford to buy the simple things in life for their own children, but a large expense like major repairs was not ok.

But the point I am still making is just of the first year some help was needed but after that the wife and I became very independent, yes we did without some things but that is how we saved money to get by and to make ends meet. My son's are the same way they watch were money and how they spend it they stand on their own two feet very well and do not need help at all.

Today I can see the work ethic my sons have they both work hard at there jobs to be the best they can be and will not let anyone walk all over them because they are good at what they do and know they can go to other companies and do better, I am so proud of them and I know they know that because I have said that to them and by the way I respect them and how they live, this does a father good and now I know they will pass it along to there children.

But do you think the wife and I would get any credit for this type of behavior you know be able to be independent not crying for help every time mother would call my sister oh no it was something I heard every time she got off the phone with my sister "poor poor thing she cannot afford this or that and your sister can not go and get a job she has to stay home and watch the babies and your brother in-law does not make enough money so I need to help them by sending them money all the time".

It was like every other week mother was sending them money for something and this was when I still lived at home I heard this all the time. After I got married who knows how much of this was going on of course I would hear about it when mother and dad would come over. It would be oh your sister has money troubles not able to buy clothes for the kids.

OK great there was a point my sister got this great idea to open her own arcade business thinking she was going to make it big with all these kids playing arcade games, and of course mother though this was the best thing in the world. Here's a though were did she get the money to open this business up HU?? Certainly not on her own always crying I do not have any money to buy anything were did this money come from this business adventure.

Oh yea mother though this was funny the kids would not go home but to the arcade store were my sister sat all day watching her store and the kids would do their home work at the store until closing of course my brother in-law was that sales men I told you about earlier never home traveling around the world so when he was home on weekends he would take care of the arcade store so my sister could be at home doing what needed to be done around the home.

So I would love to know what happened to that arcade store I got some story of how they sold it or something like that but what really happened to it I will never know but somehow I can figure out what became of the arcade store just by hearing some of the stories mother would say to dad and how they were not the same lies mother would tell other family members, come on really you must think I am really stupid! Yes my mother dose think I am stupid if they did sell it they made little or no money on it or just walked away from it not sure but one or the other.

I would like to know what would be so hard to get a part time job and work hours around your children school schedule, like my wife did she always work around their schedule my wife was always home when the kids came home from school. The one job she had for over 14 years was a crossing guard which had the same schedule the schools had and when she was done crossing she would be home the same time the boys were.

For my sister no; I would get all these kinds of excuses from my mother how hard it was to find a job were my sister lived there were no jobs' to be found!! "Really must think I am stupid or something" oh I keep saying that because that is how she made me feel.

Mother would say your poor sister cannot get jobs out there they have nothing; yah right mother lazy does not fall far from the tree! She would rather open her own business like an arcade store and pour money into it instead of saving money and getting a job even if it was just a couple times a week!! There would be more excuses like with your brother in-law traveling all the time your sister needs to be home when he is home or there will never see each other.

OH!! And I am the stupid one that graduated college with learning disabilities how do you think my wife and I made it she work hours I was home and I worked part time when she was home there were times we did not see each other for days at a time only at night when I would come home late from working part time and she was in bed sleeping she would get up just to say hi.

You see my mother never got it! Everything we did was nothing compared to my sister life everything was so perfect and so great and never did anything wrong, everything I did was never good enough but what my sister did you never heard a negative word on how she lived.

I never cared what my mother thought because I knew in my own heart what we did as husband and wife was the best for us and our way of life, yes it was hard for both of us but never any words of praise, what should I expect never got it growing up never got it in my life now or never will.

You see my wife could not understand why we would not get praise on how well we did or able to stand on our own two feet she keep expecting something she would never get and I trying telling the wife do not expect to get a word of support or praise because it will never come.

I said to my wife get praise or support from my mother is like being stranded on a deserted inland waiting to be rescued it will never come you are on your own just get use to it because will never have it.

My wife got support and praise from her parents but to my wife that was not enough she thought she was going to get it from my mother, NO I said you will not so stop looking for it I never got it from her so what makes you think you are going to get it, and mother will not denounce what my sister does no matter how bad or wrong my sister is or she does no wrong in mother eyes all we do in not good enough or worth any kind of praise.

As I said before if you are not on mother's favorite list forget it, you are not worth anything or even lessened you will be ignored and anything you say will not be respected as you know what you are talking about. This is what I lived with all the time as I lived at home, but once I moved out mother go worst, never ever having anything nice to say, but I did not have to lessen to it any more since I moved out all I had to do was just shut it out and not around to hear it but my wife could not she just did not understand.

Even when my son's graduated college or got a good job, purchase their own homes there was no praise for them or us and the best thing my son's would hear was how nice.

But for my sister's children that is all I would hear how they graduated college and what kind of job they got how wonderful it is and how much better they are. We would never do that to our kid's pick one over the other they are treated as equals this is where favorites always are better.

So what are my sisters kid's doing today well one is living in Alaska moved away and fell out of mother favoritism now she does not talk about him at all he is a bad boy moved away and does not talk to his own mother, sound kid of similar doesn't.

Well something must have happened when he came home to live with his wife and child something when wrong and of course I will never know what happened it is covered up by mother to hide and lies as she does so well and not tell you the truth about her favorite daughter who is so perfect it just her child when bad of course not my sister fault never the case.

But of course my sisters oldest son that is all I hear now of how he is doing so great living in Florida doing some kind of job not really explained what he does and living in a house or owning this house not sure of that and with roommates not married 40 something but in my mother eye's he is great perfect life, never tells me or the wife how we raised good son's respectable and hard working and is proud of them no just criticizing all the time.

How does one live and deal with that not sure how I have done it myself all my life I guess I have developed thick

skin to ignore it and turn away from the nativity that I have
had to endure all my life. Guess the way you deal with non
support and nativity and that is how I have done it is to find
your own positive support some were any were you can, for
me it was working hard and getting your support and praise
there and home with my own family or just reach around
and pat yourself on the back and tell yourself you have done
a great job.

There are so many times I go to bed at night and talk
to my God and ask him to get me thru another day give me
strength to deal with what I cannot deal with and strength
to deal with the unknown.

I believe in prayer not to many people know I have a
very strong faith in God he is someone I can turn to when
there is no one that I can and I have had a lot of that over
the years specialty after father passed. God has been I pillar
of strength because without believe in him who knows what
could of happened to me.

That is one thing I will give my parents credit for
teaching about God because his is there weather you believe
it or not. God has gotten me thru some very tough times
and I thank him all the time. I feel more people need a
little of their god in their life this would make the world be
a better place.

Chapter 7

So where do I stand today on this mother thing I have been talking about thru this whole book, well me review this with you nothing has changed it is the same today as it was at the very start and I believe even worst then before and more that my mother losses control over me.

What! you do not believe me! let me prove what I am saying today I'm over 60 years old and to this day I have been called a dummy, stupid and other names I cannot write about so let me go over some of the more direct abuse anyone would have to endure in one's life.

After father passed more than 20 years ago mother set out on her own on not talking to me about any of her affairs first it was selling the house I grew up in. Father started the process of putting it up for sale and was not going to take anything less than $250,000 for this custom built house on a ¾ acre of land when he found out he had thermal liver cancer.

Well father learned quickly that no one was going to pay that kind of money for out of date custom built home with no master bath and no large formal dining room in a home. So he started lowering his price to $230,000 but as the market would support his price was still too high. I know this because father would talk to me and he would lessen to me and as I said before we had an understanding and we could talk!

But father was fighting cancer for close to 5 years but I try not to remember that and watching father wither away to nothing before dying, but he fell very ill and the end was close mother called and said father was taken to the hospital and that he was not coming out and that we should go there I got there in time to be with father and he was almost comatose and got the chance to say good bye and father responded with I love you first time and the last time he ever said that to me it was hard to lose him but I knew he loved me he may never said that to me but I always knew it but it was nice to hear.

After fathers burial things changed for the worst, mother would not even let me know what she was doing until it was over such as the sale of fathers house mother sold it for a ridicules low price of $168,000 never told me about it until the deal was done.

I know there was no way that the house was worth selling at that price. All I got was that is what the house was worth and I could not take care of it and no one was helping me! Really mother it was late September and the lawn was about done and I would go over anytime she needed something, but mother loved to point out that I never came around to do anything.

When it came to purchasing houses and selling them the wife and I were already very knowledgeable because by this point we have purchased two homes and sold another so you think mother would confide in me or ask me some questions but mother was a know it all!

But no she did this all on her own and I know mother got bad advice from the realtor and lessened to them on what to sell the house for and of course would never ask me or the wife anything because in her mind I am too stupid to know anything about sell a home.

All I got was that is what the house was worth and I could not take care of it and no one was going to helping me! (same old story)

Ok right mother I was around to take care of the yard and anything else but no she would not let me know anything keep me in the dark mother sold everything and moved in her little town home and all I would get was you were not around to help me! Sure why not just call me and tell me you need my help.

Always making me out to be the bad guy and of course tell all of the family what a bad son I was. Yep her son does not care about his own mother, yah sure! so were was my sister in all of this no were to be found living out of state just made it in for father funeral and then gone never to return until mother 90 surprise birthday party and then when she was bed ridden after knee replacement surgery a few years ago.

But mother excuse for my sister was "Ho she as a business to run and cannot be away from it for a long time she has to work 7 days a week and 12 hour days such a tuff life owning your business"!

Yes so the only time my sister came around was to make herself look good in front of the family and she even came in for mother 90th and wow what a big deal mother made about that it was like no one did anything for her, and of course mother forgot the 80th surprise party my wife put together for her making all the arrangements and phone calls getting family and friends together for her day.

Oh yes mother never gave any praise or expectants of what was done for her, ok she said thank you mother was not that heartless but that was it! There was no over the top of any kind of appreciation or gratitude for all the work my wife had put in or what was done.

There was a lot of things my mother forgot about what my wife and I did for her, she would always bring up something that I did wrong or we fought about in the past, never ever anything we did good for her was never talked about or bought up appreciated or was thankful for.

Perfect example my wife and I came up with an idea for a surprise 50th anniversary party and paid air fare and hotel to Las Vegas so again the wife did all the work putting it together making the arrangements for the party and air fare and getting the hotel lined up.

So we called my sister and told her of the idea and of course all in for it loved the idea and said just let me know how much my half is and I will send the check. (I bet mother paid her back for her shear of the cost somehow or some way)??

The party went off without a problem and they were totally surprised and I could see dad loved the idea of going to Las Vegas but I could see mother was not too happy about going.

I have a prepared speech for mom and dad and when it came time to give that speech I stated reading it and what I wrote was funny and everyone enjoyed it but as I looked up I could see one of my ants mothers sister watching me and trying to coach me thru my speech.

Which really makes me believe that mother spread the word to everyone of how illiterate I was which really made me mad she was telling her family I was stupid and dumb any way I finish my speech and let my mom and dad say what they wanted.

When father and mother returned I talked to dad and asked how it was and of course I know I would get a straight answer from him, well he said I had a great time, gambled stayed up all night they went out to dinner.

But he did say mother was not having a good time complained about almost everything and how hot it was and of course mother was not much of a gambler or would not go with dad and or be there with him. I know myself they spent about 90% of the time away from each other.

Ask mother about the trip she never said anything nice about it or how much she appreciated what the wife and I did, it was nothing but complains about how board she was and that father was up all night gambling, there was nothing but nothing about appreciating what you did for her and how much trouble you went thru to put this party together for them.

But if my sister was mention in putting this trip together it was oh my daughter did such a great job and it was so nice what she did, it was like mother was giving my sister all the praise in the world for working so hard.

So let's get the facts right one more time my wife put this together and did all the work she made all the phone calls and arrangements for the trip plus the restaurant and work hard to make it a surprise for mother and father and all my sister had to do was mail in her half of the cost for everything.

There was no appreciation for this no nothing from mother, but dad was very happy and appreciated what my wife did and what she went thru to put this together and thanked us for what we did.

So when mother says how much my wife was trouble and such a bad person and made her life so miserable and caused all this trouble mother just seems to forget or does not want to remember what my wife did for her for over the 35 years we have been married and all the parties and arrangements this person did for her.

Also I am not saying my wife is perfect and the best daughter in-law there is but she did things for my mother and no one had to ask her to do this she just did it because she wanted to and yes my wife wanted some recognition for being a good daughter in-law.

But that was not going to happen I never got any recognition all my life for the things I did and accomplished and have become as a person you think my mother would ever say how proud she was of me or anything like that all I got was insulted, emasculated, and lied to all my life and never ever was praised for anything I have become or did in my life plus how much I knew about anything in life or how smart I really was and how much smarter I was over my mother.

I tried telling my wife don't look of it and you will never get any kind of praise so if you expect to get it you are going to wait a long time and never receive it so if you want any kind of recognition you are not going to get it, many of times she could not understand it and many times I tried telling her it was not going to come.

So here is a list of some things we did for mother that she always seems to forget what was done for her and never have had a special thank you for doing anything this is also to let my family know I am not a bad son or she has a bad daughter in-law.

1. Arranged a surprise 50th anniversary party with an all expenses paid air fare and hotel trip to Las Vegas for mother and father.

2. Arranged for a surprise 80th birthday party for mother after father had passed.

3. Invited mother over for every holiday, mother's day, father's day, birthday, graduation, and any party we were having at our house after father had passed.

4. After mother had sold their house and moved into her town home I would go over to her place and fix and repair anything that needed fixing.

5. Plus as mother got older the wife and I would be running over to her place to take her to the doctors, take her shopping and help clean after she came back from the nursing home when mother had her knee replaced or broke her ankle, fell and broke her wrist, and her tale bone.

This may sound like any other family member that should take care of their own mother or father, and you are right this is my responsibly to take care of her. I never ever neglected my responsibly to run over to her house to do something for her and take care of her so do not think I am that type of person.

But I am pointing out all I have done for my mother was never acknowledged or appreciated anything we did for her all I would received is mother would say "you never did anything for me or take care of anything for me you would not come over to take my garbage out or stop by I would have to call you all the time" everything just was thrown in my face as a son that did nothing but try to be a good son and never told her family or friends what I did for her but mother would tell everyone how bad I was and how bad her daughter in-law was.

Yes I am not a saint let's get that clear and I do not clam to be one but no child should have to endure this kind of abuse. I have made it a point to be nothing like my mother to my children I make sure I appreciate everything they do and I make sure I tell them that too and the family how good my son's are and that I appreciate them.

As parents or so to be parents take a lesson from this book do not be like this to your children they will resent you for ever and as I talked about giving your children praise, support and true love you will receive appreciation and love in return many times over.

Again I want to go over something to prove a point of how my own mother has put me down, emasculated me, insulted me and lied to me all my life. Witch I believe was to manipulate, control and to hide things from me to make me fell stupid, insignificant, and worthless, and my mother wonders why I did not like being around her because I never received a kind word.

Plus I believe this was also to hide real things from me about my sister and how bad off she really is, and to make it sound as she is so great and I am so bad and stupid that would never know anything about what is going on with my sister and her financial life style.

Because my mother gave her support all her married life by not only sending her money, but when we were invited to a graduations, birthday parts, anniversary, and holidays to give a gift to for these events because of we are very close families mother would buy the gift or put money in a envelop and say it was from my sister and then lie and side that her daughter mailed the gift to my house and had mother bring it and use the reason she lives out of state!

How stupid does my mother thing I am I was there to see everything and even heard mother say this to me, my sister never sent mother the money to cover anything mother did for her, she did not want my sister to look bad in front of the family, because I know she would never send anything to anybody on either side of the family and my own sister never sent anything to my kids for there birthdays, graduations, or Christmas.

Of course my sister wants to look good now that my son's are married and having children of there own, now my sister is sending something to them, but she gets this tuff for free and embroidering there names on it to make her look good and make it look like she is spending a lot of money, I know this because my son's told me this they said to me that look what your sister sent us she told us that was left from a previous order and that had extra so she embroidered our names on it and sent it to us.

Again trying to look good in front of the family which she never did before, but if I tried this and asked mother to do this for me because we could not afford it or did not have the money to give a gift, I would never hear the end of it she would insult and bagger me for days and never let me forget it but my poor sister it was ok to buy a gift for her or put money in an envelop for her, but that is OK!

Being over 60 years old and have graduated college, traveled all over the United States and Europe, taken small classes and been to finance meetings and seminars, purchased and sold 5 homes, been a landlord with rental homes for over 12 years, plus have had over 21 years in business purchasing in the manufacturing industry for company's worth tens of millions of dollars, I would say I am pretty knowledgeable man.

The reason I am pointing the above accomplishments out is that for someone with learning disabilities and having trouble in school I have come a long way to be a respectable person and a hard working individual which has spilled over on my own son's and they are very accomplished people themselves.

To this day when it comes for my mother to make very important or critical decisions in life you think my mother would confide in me or ask me the questions of what to do or how to do, but NO I am the last person on earth she would talk to or ask for advice, and when I wanted to tell her that I knew more about a subject or have done the very thing she is doing then all she does is get this loud NO, NO, NO!!! You do not know anything this is what is right because my friend, family member or someone else said this is the right way to do this.

Here is a perfect example mother did not know anything about the world of economics or business, the wife and I want to purchase property in another state the one place we both loved the most was Las Vegas NV.

So we contacted our local real estate agent and they gave us a good agent in Las Vegas to help us, so we went out there and started the process of viewing homes for potential rental property, and after 2 days we found the perfect place it was in a gated community, two story townhome with three bedrooms.

Why did I want to purchase property out of state! This was a plan of mine to rent the property and have someone else pay my mortgage and in time make the townhome a vacation home and when I was ready to retire this would be perfect place I could move in and retire if I so desired.

Of course everything did not go as well as expected, there is always a learning curve to anything you do in life, that is how you grow as a person and you learn quickly, we did with our first management company that we hired to rent the town home they were not very good and did not rent the property and home went vacant for months, so I fired them and I went on line and found another really good company which got the property rented in a few weeks we were very happy with them and keep them as our property management company for over 8 years.

Well when mother hear of some of the problems we were having with our rental property such as not rented yet or we need to send in the landscaper to clean up the yard, mother would give me that bitchy face and say in such a deeming and insulting tone, "why do you have to have another place in Las Vegas like that you should sell it and get ride of it and flip it like your ant, you do not know what you are doing by having a place out of state"!

The same kind of insults mother gave me when I was looking to find a job as a teenager, never giving me and my wife any kind of credit for thinking outside the box and planning for ones future. As I have told my wife before that I felt mother was jealous of us having more or being better and even smarter with money then my sister who lived on a shoe string and living pay check to pay check.

So when the wife and I decided to purchase a second rental property in Arizona a year later we were not going tell mother at all what we did until we found a place to buy.

Again we when to our local real state agent and they got us in touch with one in Goodyear Arizona which we heard it was an up and coming suburb of Phoenix, after looking for two days we again found a new subdivision starting up and found a three bedroom patio home we made the purchase and the next day before we left to back home we went to the design center and picked out everything for the house in a mater of an hour.

Why because we had a plane to catch because our time on vacation was over, so as the months went on the house was being built and I started the process of looking for a management company to take care of the home and get it rented. I had found one management company that was recommended so I called them up and we got the process started which they got the home rented in about a month.

By this time mother had found out we purchased a second home and she was now furious she was more deeming and insulting then ever. Who would think a parent would not be more supportive to the child and not insulting. I think jealousy was the big part it was that I could do something my sister could not do or even they mother hated I was better than her and my sister.

I believe because of mother not finishing high school and not understanding what business is all about or even understand what we were doing and why, plus even lessening to me and try to see what we were doing and why we did this.

Yet again all I got was that bitchy face and start at me of how could you do this and what are you thinking you are doing something smart you do not know what you are doing.

Ok parents how many of you do this to your own children never support them and understand why they are doing what they do and for what reason, how many of you support your children and give them guidance help when they need it, I will bet a lot of you because you love your children and what them to succeed in life and do well and you know what business is all about and knowledge of the economy.

All my mother knows was insults and jealousy because we were smarter with our money then my sister and brother in-law were and could have more then them, mother did not want us to have anything better then my sister and to believe I knew more then her or then anyone else and that I did have a brain in my head and that I was successful.

I talk about these things because of what type of person I have become; I had to work very hard at being the best at something and succeeding weather I have my mothers approval or support or not, this has been said before early in my book if no one pats you on the back then reach around and pat yourself on the back look in the mirror and tell yourself good job, be proud of yourself and support your own ideas.

If you do not have thick skin then develop thick skin because if you do not you will fall pray to the insults and ridicule for other and you will dough yourself into felling you can not do anything or be anybody even to sauced in life so let the insults and ridicule roll off your back.

Do not give up on your dreams make your choices good or bad you have to fall down in order to learn how to get up. Then when you get up you know your mistake and do not do it again you have to be mentally tuff when someone tells you that you cannot do that or your do not have the ability to be achieve your goals, this is your bell to come out swinging harder and stronger then ever.

Just remember no one did anything for me no one gave me support, encouragement, love, and understanding, everyone tried to stop me insult me and made me fell insignificant about myself.

That is went I dough deep inside and look at myself and side you can do anything you put your mind to, and you know what I did it with out help or support, and when you fall on your face get up and keep digging with a never give up attitude and you will succeed and get the golden ring you can then shove it in the doubters face and say see I did it with out your help.

Even thou they will not acknowledge your accomplishments and give you your just dues or praise, you will know yourself you succeed at something and then you can rub it in the doubters face and it is your own satisfaction that you accomplished something you set out to do.

Manny times my own mother tried to knock me down by telling I could not do what I want to do especially when I went to college I knew mother had no confidence in me to finish, there was not support or go and do it attitude, mother did not think I could of graduated a junior college but I did which surprised her and then when I went to a four year university to finish mother never knew how hard it was on me and going on probation twice which she never knew about.

But I got thru it no matter how difficult it was and no matter how hard I had to work for it, I did it with out any of her praise or support not even encouragement.

The day I graduated college was one of the best days of my life at that point and there was such a feeling of accomplishment, when they gave me my diploma I held it high in the air as if I was shoving in the face's of all the people and my mother who doubted me, making a statement look what I did something you insinuated me with and that I was not smart enough to do, but look what I did something you could not do.

Ok so I sound as if I want revenge for all the bad things that happened to me and what I went thru in life, not true this is about standing up when you get knocked having a strong will that will not let you down, not letting anyone or anything stand in your way of accomplishing your goals or finishing what you started.

This is about being mentally strong, and when someone tells you that you cannot, you show them you can. I am living proof of being so mentally strong that when anyone gives me dough or tells me you will not succeed this is when I get very focused on the target.

I like giving examples this is how I have to prove my point and there are dozens of examples that I can give and have proven of how mentally strong I am, and the one example that really stands above all other accomplishments this is when I lost my job in March of 2013, that was right in the middle of my father in-law passing and the wife was having an estate and garage sale and I was helping with the sale everyday and I had little time to find a job because of being over at the in-laws house and running around left me almost no time to look for a job.

Many times I would just go over to the in-laws with the wife and help them set up and then I would go home and jump on the computer and start looking for a job and I would all day job hunting and then send out as many as 20 resumes in one day then about 4pm run back to my in-laws house and help them close up.

The next day I would spend at the in-laws house working I would receive a couple of phone calls regarding my resume they received then there would be a phone interview and sometimes I would get an appointment to go in for an interview.

This would go on for months over the spring and summer; I was not going to give up for any reason and was determined to find a new job and fast. Of course interview after interview a new position fell thru and seemed nothing was going to happen I could see this was warring on my wife and she was getting upset with all these phone calls and interviews nothing was happening but I was not going to give up, most of all letting my mother know I failed at getting a job this is what she always wanted is to see me fall down and fail so she could say I told you so! But of course mother would never say that to my face but the innuendos were there and I could hear them when I would talk to her about my job search and how it was going.

You ask what kind of innuendos that she would say to me that would make me think she felt like that, first would be the tone of her voice it would change when mother would find out that an interview I went on that a second interview did not happen or I would get a dear John email, (this I what I called them when a company would send me an email thanking me for the interview and how much they enjoyed talking to me and my interest in there company but my qualifications were not just what they were looking for) any one out of work looking for work will know what I am talking about.

When I talk about my mother voice changing it was not of a disappointed voice for me it would be a sarcastic type of voice and I would not get anything like you will get the next one, or they do not know what they are missing in not hiring you or even telling not to give up but hang in there.

It was more like the too bad type voice that I would get and then she would say something like well there are not too many jobs out there and there are some many people out of work you may have to take what every you can get just for an income. This was kind of writing me off as if you will not get as good as a job you had or it would sound as if she was say you failed in school and you will fail at getting a job too.

But I have said this to my wife many times that I would rather kill myself then letting my mother have the satisfaction of knowing I would not get a new job or failing at something, and that I would do whatever it took to succeed at finding a job or anything I did in life and not let her have that satisfaction know I failed.

This I something that haunts me every day of my life knowing my mother just sits and waits for me to fail at something and will enjoy watching my fail and fall down and become something mother though that I would always be a failure.

Call it whatever you want determination, ego or self pride I will not fail or give up on anything I do in life. Yes everybody fails and so do I but I will not give up at anything I do, yes I will fail but I will keep failing until a goal is accomplished and I will not stop till I succeed weather I never get support from mother or not I will support myself and succeed at anything I put my mind to it.

So back to my story of succeeding, in late June I received one of those phone interviews and was told there would be another phone call setting up a personal interview.

Receiving that phone call within an hour of talking to that person on the phone we set up a time to meet with a schedule of people to talk to. After arriving at the interview talking to 6 people and spending over 6 hours with this company putting everything I had into this interview.

I started the interview with the VP of sourcing and ended with him we talked for another 15 minutes then we finished with the VP telling me that they have a few more people to talk to before making a decision and that I would hear from them in a week or so.

Ok I said we shook hands and left figure about a week after the fourth of July maybe I will hear something, when I got home I sent thank you emails to all the people I talked to and when on looking of a job.

To finish this up I receive a phone call on July 8th and it was HR manager and she said they like me and wanted to make an offer. There was nothing more than that I wanted to hear and the rest is history.

I could not wait to call mother and tell her HA, HA I received a job offer and better position then what I was doing I am not a senior buyer anymore I was offered a purchasing managers position.

So as a parent we are very happy for your children when they succeed at what every they do weather a new job, promotion, graduating college, getting a masters or even purchasing an new home.

Your voice shows it with happiness, joy, and even sounding proud of them, but I never got that and never got it before what makes me think I will get it now plus I never received an ounce of praise before growing up and now that I am a man of over 60 years old I still do not know what this is like getting any praise from my own mother, the voice she use it was a voice that sounded jealous or even envious that I did even better than expected.

So all mother would say "oh that is nice is the job far from home" and of course she want to hear I will have to drive hours to get there, but no I said less than a half hour away, and I would hear that voice again saying "that's nice making the same amount of money?" no making more! And that was the dagger that did her in and that voice got even more envious and jealous "well I bet you have to work more hours and have more responsibly" I said yes it dose mother I will be there manager and yes there is more responsibly but I will work 8 to 5pm.

As this was discussed earlier in my book a child needs to hear this from their parents as sense of pride or being proud of making the child fell good about themselves, but what is that like for me I will never know I never got that from my mother and never will, father showed me he was proud but never really saying that to me was still something I wanted to hear as a child or as an adult it is something I will never know how that feels that a parent is proud of their child making them feel good about themselves.

So how does someone go thru life not knowing how it feels and how does it affect them into their life not getting any kind of support or praise I kind word even some kind of love.

For someone who lived thru it this was and is still very difficult thing to live with, there are times of low self a steam, no confidence in myself to want to do anything or even try to do anything that is remotely difficult or even time consuming.

This is where I have to force myself to get up and do it weather it was running for trustee, getting involved at our church, or having special project in my carrier that needs doing, simple tasks are a chore for me.

I am afraid of failure plan and simple there is nothing worst then failing not achieving ones goals, I had to be mentally strong, and so strong that nothing gets in my way of doing what I need to do to complete anything I start and plus not be afraid of failure.

Because failure makes you better everybody fails as something in there life everyone and you need to embrace failure as a learning tool as you fail you get better at what you are doing and you stop failing and then you start seceding and excelling.

So when someone who tells you they never fail at anything and whatever they do they seceded and excel at everything, well they are lying to your face. When someone tells you that you can look at these kinds of people and ask them ever play a computer game? If they say yes you can then say "will I guess you made it thru the whole game without getting stopped or dying HU".

Because I have seen the best video game players not even get out of the first level before they die and the start over to the point where they made their mistake and fix that mistake and move on to the next level and die again.

Life is like a video game but not a game at all but a serious of levels in one's life you will need to get by before you can move on, like school each grade is a level you make some mistakes fix them and move on to finish your grade get your passing grade and move on to the next level "grade"

You make mistakes along the way but you do not lose your focus on the finial prize and this is passing your grade to move on to the next grade.

After you graduate school, college or graduate school, your next level is getting a job and carrier you always wanted and excelling at it, sure you will make your share of mistakes to but you learn from them and you get better at your job and then get promoted or find a better job and move on to you next level.

So without any kind of support, praise or even a well done it is hard to get past those levels I have talked about, you have to learn how to fall down and get up and sometimes with help you can get better and with support you get that push and determination that you can have that never give up attitude that keeps you going and moving to meet your goal or goals in life.

I have said this before in this book and I will say it again, there has never been a time in my life from my parents of outright support and what I have been talking about is your parent come to your side for reinsurance, help, love and understanding.

Father would give me that look of support and a few words of support but that was about it, and this was sometimes all I needed, but still how about real support which I never ever got from mother all I received was insults or degraded if I feel down or stumbled.

But somehow that fueled my fire to succeed and to reach my goal no matter what is was, being in college and struggling to get off probation it took me a few terms but I did it!! and I would rather died then give my mother any kind of satisfaction knowing I failed and looking at her giving me that look of I told you so!

So in some way I should thank mother for giving me this level of determination and this never say die attitude with a will that cannot be broken, NA!! I would never give her that satisfaction or give her the acknowledgement she was in any way shape or form part of my success in life.

So mother if you read my book you were never an inspiration to me at all, only father was the biggest inspiration to me in how I lived my life, father thought me how to be a hard working individual and that no one was ever going to give me anything unless you worked hard for it.

Plus one more thing father thought me is that you need to take care of number 1, and that is you and you alone, why? Because no one else will take care of you, and you do not look for anyone to do that because it will not happen and the second thing is you take care of is your family.

Perfect example is you lose your job, who is going to help you get a new one, NO body! This is what happened to me I went out and looked for a new job sent resumes made phone calls, and even to suppliers I knew to give me referrals or letters of recommendations, but you have to get the interviews yourself, no one will help you and I have seen my letters of recommendations get dismissed, so just remember no one will help you but you alone.

The same with school who will help you gradate no one only you, yes you can get help to study or get a tutor to help with class you are having trouble in, but who will do the work and take the test it is you. Plus you have to ask for help no one will give it to you no one and you have to work hard for that passing grad the test is on you right!

Writing this book I am not trying to get back at anyone but so show what I went thru in my life and how I got thru it and still being a good person I cannot be evil to people because it is not in me to be that way I feel you should treat people the way you would like to be treated and with God in my life it helps because I believe maybe not everyone does but people can be good weather they do or not.

Sure some people may think I am a bad son with no respect and even tell me how could you write this story about your mother this way, she is a good person she gave birth to you raised you and took care of you and loved you.

Yes they may think they are right but again I say you never saw mother for who she really was you only got one side of the story and one side of the lies. If you lived with her you would of know her wrath of how we were all treated me, dad and her daughter.

Oh yes my sister, mothers favorite but my sister could not stand mother at all remember she could not wait to get married and move far away from her, just as she told me as things were getting set for the wedding. But now my mother is living with my sister in Georgia paying her bills and buying her a new home to live in.

The only reason this arrangement is like this is because my sister is in financial trouble and mother needs to bail her out! And of course family members will call me a liar and I am making it up and this book is about sour grapes.

Again I say to them, no it is not about sour grapes it is about being treated as a son and a child who has done everything for his mother he could his whole life and go nothing for it but grief, insults, emasculation and no support thru my life but ended standing on his own two feet to be the best person he could be with no help from no one.

As an adult I have missed having the support of a parent just once I would of like to hear I am proud of you son or we will support you even being told you can be whatever you want to be and helping me believe in myself.

But missing this in life makes a person fell left alone and unwanted as I state "I was a mistake in ever being born" watching other parents embrace their children with love and respect after achieving a goal or trying hard and not finish first they are there to put their arm around there child and say good job you gave it your best do not worry you will get them next time just keep trying.

What does that feel like? I do not know and I will never know how that feels, but my son's know how that feels because I was that type of parent sportive, encouraging, loving, believing in them and just being there for them.

So as I finish this book I would like to remind parents your children are a gift from a higher being weather you believe in God or any other God our children are a gift and we should love them no matter what, they need our love and support all the time never stop, never quite loving your children because they are special.

Printed in the United States
By Bookmasters